Larger Trout
for the
Western Fly Fisherman

From West Yellowstone, Montana, Dec. 22, 1983.

Rick Murphy

Larger Trout
for the
Western Fly Fisherman

By

Charles E. Brooks

NICK LYONS BOOKS
WINCHESTER PRESS

Produced by
NICK LYONS BOOKS
212 Fifth Avenue
New York, NY 10010
Published and distributed by
WINCHESTER PRESS
New Century Publishers, Inc.
220 Old New Brunswick Road
Piscataway, NJ 08854
PRINTED IN THE UNITED STATES OF AMERICA
10 9 8 7 6 5 4 3 2 1

Library of Congress Cataloging in Publication Data

Brooks, Charles E., 1921-
      Larger trout for the western fly fisherman.

      "A Nick Lyons book."
      Includes index.
      1. Trout fishing.   2. Fly fishing.   I. Title.
SH687.B83   1983   799.1'755   83-3532
ISBN 0-8329-0329-9

TO GRACE

Secretary, typist, financial agent, chauffeur, critic, fellow researcher, dry fly fisherman, and wife of 23 years, without whose nagging "get something into my work basket" it might never have been finished, this book is affectionately dedicated.

Contents

Introduction

This book has been written for the experienced fly fisherman. In it, I have assumed that the reader will have long ago accumulated sufficient basic tackle, and learned how to cast well enough to suit his purpose.

The same holds for leader selection, the proper knots to use, and other rudiments and fundamentals that one should learn by the end of his first year as a fly fisherman.

In this book the reader will soon learn that I have not hesitated to include my personal opinions. These opinions did not spring full blown into life. The material herein represents what I have learned in my thirty-five years of trout fishing experience, at least twenty years of which involved diligent research. This book has been over fifteen years in the writing.

In my research, I laid hold of all the ideas, opinions, theories and facts that I could find—or that I became aware of. I sifted and checked, thrashed and winnowed. I read several hundred books on the subject. The conclusions I reached are presented here. None of them were lightly arrived at. Some of them are at variance with what is generally accepted. In some cases, it is expected that some anglers will take violent exception to some conclusions.

All I can say is that the research and study were most carefully done, and good instruments and my most considered judgment were used. I was never interested in proving or disproving a particular theory; I merely wanted to know why, and in what manner, that theory affected the fishing. A good many of my own cherished ideas came a cropper as a result of careful study.

All the research in the world will never succeed in reducing fly fishing to an exact science. This, I suppose, is because fish behavior is as individualistic as human behavior. When some psychologist comes around and says he understands human behavior completely, and proves it, I may concede that the same is possible with fish. At that time I will also give up fishing. It would cease to be fun.

I have several times repeated the same thing in this book, namely that it is imperative that the wet fly fisherman get his fly down to the *bottom* of the stream if he wishes to make consistent catches of good trout.

Although such repetition might seem unnecessary, my experience has led me to believe otherwise. I have instructed scores of fishermen in wet fly usage—intelligent men and experienced anglers. Invariably, I have found that all of them, without exception, considered the fly to be on the bottom if it was eighteen inches to two feet below the surface, and this regardless of the depth of the hold. I constantly had to admonish these anglers: *"Keep the fly on the bottom. If you do not feel it touch bottom now and then You are not fishing deep enough!"*

I cannot find words to describe how difficult it is to convince anglers that their fly is not on the bottom. Nor am I alone in this feeling, one angler I knew had instructed fly fishing in a boys' camp for over forty years. He told me he found it so difficult to convey this important point that he had resorted to the following demonstration at the beginning of every class: Taking his students to the head of a medium run about eighteen inches deep, he would toss in a handful of bright colored flies of the size commonly used in the area. These unattached flies would drift with the current and he and the students would follow along the bank. When the flies started to catch to the bottom, he would wade out and retrieve them, then point out the distance that they had traveled before reaching the bottom. It varied from thirty to forty *feet*.

Even after the above demonstration, he said, he constantly had to remind the students to cast more directly upstream, and to drop the fly well above the expected lie of the fish.

Therefore, I do not believe this particular point can be overemphasized, especially since I firmly believe that all that separates the average wet fly angler from the very good one, in most cases, is the *depth at which the fly is fished.*

I have attempted to avoid writing of those methods and practices, which are in common use, and descriptions of which have appeared in countless books. By refraining from mentioning them, I do not wish it to appear as if I condemn them. It is just that I believe them so widely used and so well known that no further mention of them is needed.

What I have attempted is to present other, less widely known, but very effective practices, methods, flies, and presentations. While every angler will not care to use all the tactics and techniques outlined here, I believe that there will be one or more which many anglers have not tried, and which, if used, will add to their success.

I have made references to large catches several times in this volume. Nearly all these fish were returned to the water uninjured. I have no quarrel with the man who takes and keeps a limit of fish. If he, like most, gets to fish only occasionally, it would be unreasonable to wish otherwise. I do not approve of taking and keeping large catches to give away, or throw away. In the home in which I was brought up, greed and waste were cardinal sins. They still are as far as I'm concerned.

Angling is for enjoyment, and any research connected with it should also be enjoyed. The pleasure connected with fly fishing can almost always be increased by knowing more about it. If some readers are provoked by some of my ideas to the point that they do a vast amount of research and then write a book which proves me wrong, good. I should be among the first to buy a copy of the book and to congratulate the author. I hope someone writes such a book.

Introduction to the 1983 Edition

In the thirteen years since the first edition of this book was published, fly fishing and the conservation and protection of trout waters has grown faster and to a greater degree than at any time in the history of our sport.

All facets of the sport have progressed. We have now fly lines that will do anything the fisherman desires. Rods have been improved in both quality (action and line handling) and material. Though it may cause some bamboo lovers to leap up in rage, graphite makes a better rod. Leaders are far better now than they were in 1970. Fly-tying materials have burgeoned; a hundred—no, five hundred—dry-fly-quality blue-dun necks are available now for every one in 1970. We have scores of fly tyers of the very top class now tying flies for the trade.

The fishing has improved, from the standpoint that we now have more sensible regulations, better stream management, more and stronger safeguards against mindless stream destruction, many fly-fishing-only waters, more catch-and-release waters.

There are now two firms engaged in trout-stream reclamation, both founded out of information in this and another of my books. States doing trout-habitat improvement now number in double figures. Senseless stocking of hatchery catchables has been largely stopped in naturally productive waters in most states. Things are better for the trout fisherman in all respects than they were in 1970, and they will continue to get better because of the great number of keen, environmentally conscious young men and women joining the ranks of fly fishers.

But one thing has not changed: our beloved quarry, the trout. Trout are still as moody and difficult as they ever were—in fact, with the education of catch-and-release fishing helping things along, they may be even more difficult. Hurray for that! If fishing for trout ever gets easy, we'd all give it up. We go fishing because we hope to catch fish, but we all know that the actual catching is only a small part of a rich, varied, often frustrating but somehow rewarding experience that I believe is unsurpassed among the pleasures of this earth.

None of the material in this book has been changed by any of the above. It is as valid today as it was the day it was written, because it was written with the trout, its habits and habitat in mind, and to inform the angler about those, with the hope it would improve his or her angling. I have corrected only a few printer's errors and added new photographs and captions.

I've always believed that knowing more about something increases one's pleasure. I hope the information in this book will increase yours in fly fishing for trout.

CHARLES E. BROOKS
West Yellowstone, Montana

[1]

The Language of Fly Fishing

H. H. "Dike" Smedley, in his book *Trout of Michigan,* bemoaned the fact that terms for flies, both artificial and natural, are so loosely used by fishermen as to confuse even the most informed. He doesn't mention other fishing terms, but anyone who has read much on fly fishing has now and then run into a term that stumps him, at least in the manner in which it is used.

It has been so since men started to write of fishing for sport. In *The Origins of Angling,* John McDonald's footnotes bear witness to the fact that many of the terms used in the *Treatise on Fishing with an Angle* are puzzling. The same thing may be said of books and articles written on fishing today.

The reason, of course, is that writers seldom give a thought to the fact that a term commonplace to them may not be so to anyone else, or that a term commonly used in their area may be unknown, or have a different meaning elsewhere.

Sectional differences in definition are widespread in the U. S.: what is considered "Trout" in one section may mean a fish known as a bass in another. "Native Trout," a term commonly used in both eastern and western United States, means two different fish— the brook trout in the east and the cutthroat in the west.

Particularly confusing are the terms for various parts of a stream, or the stream itself. Flow, pool, riffle, brook, burn, creek, bogan, stickle, run; these occur again and again in angling literature, and their usage varies with different writers. Not important? How can you concentrate on fishing a riffle if you don't know what a riffle is? I've questioned a number of anglers as to what they thought a riffle was, and have gotten three or four definitions, all of which describe completely different types of water.

I've come upon the term stickle in several angling books, yet I have never found an angler who knew exactly what type of water it meant. Nor do my several dictionaries contain any definition for the word, which could be applied to a trout stream. Consequently, when I read that "here was as sweet a stickle for trout as ever graced a stream," the writer might be fishing in a briar patch for all I know.

I have attempted herein to stay away from confusing terms, or from using words that might be misunderstood. I have particularly attempted to avoid using the various terms describing the short span of a mayfly's life, and which appear frequently in angling writing. I am referring to the terms dun, drake, spinner, brown, etc., which as far as I am concerned are completely useless in telling me what I need to know. Also, I have attempted not to use scientific terms where unnecessary to do so.

Some of the terms in this book will be used incorrectly, according to exact usage. I am well aware that crane fly larvæ are not "nymphs." But all underwater insect forms are known generally by that term by most anglers. Therefore, it is so used here.

No matter how carefully one attempts to avoid using confusing terms, some such terms must be used simply because they are inextricably woven into angling and there is no way to avoid using them without lengthy explanation. However, to prevent confusing the reader any more than necessary, I have set forth the definitions of some commonly misunderstood terms *as they are used in this book*.

Angler. Angler equals fly fisherman in this book.

Below. Downstream of the point of reference.

Broad. A wider, slower moving stretch of a stream.

Brook. Any stream averaging less than fifteen feet wide throughout its fishable length.

Caddis flies. The adult insect whose underwater life is spent in a small tube or "house" of tiny bits of stick, rush, or sand grains. Sometimes called sedge.

Cased Caddis or Caddis Nymph. The underwater form of the above.

Crane flies. A fly, very similar in appearance to a huge mosquito.

Body thin, legs very long and thin. Some call it gallanipper or mosquito hawk.

Creek. A running stream with year around flow, of less than thirty feet average width in the section under consideration. The upper reaches of a large river might be referred to as a creek in this text, since the term will be used herein to identify running streams of a certain size, regardless of the known name of the stream. For instance, the South Fork of the Madison River will be mentioned as a creek, because this is a small stream, barely thirty feet wide at the point where it enters Hebgen Lake.

Damsel flies. Similar to the dragon fly, except more slender, and the wings extend along the back when the insect is lit. Called Darning Needle and other names.

Dead water. Water that is neither holding nor feeding water, and therefore contains no fish. Never used to mean still water.

Dragon flies. Those large, long bodied flies with two pairs of horizontally extended wings, which flit around the edges of water. Called Snake Doctor and other names. The immature underwater form is about one and one-half inches long, and one-half-inch broad.

Feeding Water. Areas of the stream in which trout feed periodically, but in which they do not stay unless feeding. This is the second most important term in trout fishing. As mentioned, many streams have large feeding areas to which the trout move when on the feed, and it is important that the angler recognize these places in order not to be fishing in water that contains no trout.

In general, strictly feeding water will be relatively shallow, of good current flow, and supplied with small rocks or vegetation which furnish cover for trout food. The lower ends of runs, rapids, glides, and riffles are usually good feeding water. Cover must be present not too far away, or the trout in these areas will feed only at night. As mentioned, holding water may also be feeding water, but if so, holding water will be the term used, being the more important.

Fish flies. A fly similar in appearance to the dobson fly and the giant stone fly, somewhat smaller, and with feathery appearing antennae. Nymph smaller, but very similar to the helgramite and not too different from some stone fly nymphs.

Glide. A smooth topped section of somewhat swifter than average current.

Gliding run. Of slightly less current speed than a run, and with few obstructions.

Heavy Water. A very strong current of thigh depth or deeper, unobstructed.

Helgramite. The underwater immature form of the dobson fly, *Corydalis cornuta.*

Hold. An area of a stream known always to contain fish.

Holding Water. The most important term in trout fishing. All success in trout fishing is directly dependent upon the angler's being able to recognize holding water. It is a section or area of any stream containing those elements so vital to a trout's shelter and/or protection. Protection from his enemies, including man, is the first requirement of any trout; food will always be secondary in his survival scheme. Therefore, holding water is the term that describes the actual abode of the trout, the place where he lies throughout the day, except possibly when feeding. Ideally, holding water should be feeding water, and there are areas in most streams where this is true. However, many streams have large areas of feeding water, but few holding places; trout in such streams are invariably night feeders. It is difficult to describe holding water. There are literally thousands of spots, all different in appearance, that can be termed holding water. But one of the three following items will always be present: 1.) Something for the trout to get under, whether a rock, a log, a drift, an undercut bank or perhaps mud in which the trout can hide himself. In other words, cover. 2.) Water sufficiently deep so that the bottom is not readily visible. 3.) A broken surface, which does not allow the fish to be seen from above, and conversely, does not allow the trout to see above the surface, on it, perhaps, but not above it.

Some holding water will contain all three of the above, that is, cover, depth, and a broken surface. If this area also happens to be in the main current flow, it becomes feeding water as well, and will invariably contain trout of larger than average size for that stream.

Left bank. The bank to the left when one is facing downstream.

Lie. A spot in a stream wherein a fish is known or suspected to be. Specifically, it means that area through which you intend to move your fly, with the knowledge or expectation a fish will be able to see it.

Mayflies. The adult and semi-adult flying form (called imago and sub-imago) of the families including, but not limited to, Ephemera and Ephemerella.

Midcurrent. In the approximate middle of the main current flow.

Midge. Any tiny fly habitually seen near the surface of the water.

Midstream. Halfway between the stream banks.

Midwater. Halfway between top and bottom of a stream.

Nymph. Unless further identified, this will be used as a general term for any of the immature forms of any insect laying eggs that hatch under water. This includes, but does not limit the term to, caddis, dobson flies, mayflies, dragon and damselflies, crane flies, fish flies, and stone flies. These also may be referred to by the above names.

Pocket. A section of smoother topped water in a larger section of broken water. Usually found below (downstream) of an obstruction, or where the water suddenly deepens.

Pool. Similar to a broad but of considerable depth. Includes the deepest sections of the stream.

Rapid. A section of a stream in which there are sufficient obstructions and in which the current moves at sufficient speed to create white water over at least one half the surface.

Riffle. A shallow section not more than 18 inches deep, with the exception of possible small spots of deeper water. The bottom will be of stones of buckshot to grapefruit size, in general, and the current will be swifter than average. The surface is usually broken, but with little or no white water.

Right bank. The bank to the right when one is facing downstream.

River. Any stream which averages over thirty feet wide in the section under discussion, and up to and including the largest running streams.

Run. A section wherein the speed of the current is faster than the average and where white water exists where the current meets obstructions.

Source. (of a stream) A spring or the highest reaches of a major tributary of the stream mentioned.

Spring. A source of water which emerges from the earth.

Stone flies. Specifically refers to the giant stone fly, *Pteronarcys californica,* others of the pteronarcys group, and only rarely to any of the smaller stone flies. When the natural insect is meant, it will almost always be californica. Called willow flies and salmon flies. Nymph frequently called helgramite.

Tongue or current tongue. A secondary or minor current pushing into or separating from a main or larger current.

[2]

Holding Water and Feeding Water

Several years ago, along a tributary of the Pilgrim River in Alaska, I was instructing a friend in the art of wet fly usage. He had progressed to the point of casting well, fishing the cast out properly, and striking correctly; but his knowledge of fishing was virtually nonexistent. City born and bred, he was completely uninformed in streamcraft.

There were many areas of dead water in the stream, which was small and swift. Therefore we walked past much more water than we fished.

"Cast there," I would say, pointing to a spot, "there should be a fish there."

He would cast, and invariably get a strike. Sometimes, after he had caught one or two fish from the same spot, I would direct him to cast back to the place, saying "there should be another one there." And there usually was.

That night after supper, before the fire, pulling on our drinks, he asked, "How is it that you know right where the fish are and how many are there? How does one learn that a fish is there, even when it cannot be seen?"

It was the first time I had ever thought about it. Brought up in the wilderness, I learned to fish and walk at about the same time. The streams I fished were clear water streams, and I lived on and in them as a boy, fishing and swimming.

Of more than average curiosity, and even at an early age an avid fisherman, it was natural that I should spend many hours observing as well as fishing. I never consciously sought to "study" the fish, I was interested and watched them when not fishing.

These fish were not trout, but even so I noticed that they were never far from safety, in the form of cover or depth. Thus, as naturally as learning to walk, I learned to associate cover and depth with fish. I learned, too, that the fish were in entirely different places in the stream at night than in the daytime, and that they fed more readily then. Another bit of lore was added to my fund, without my being aware of it, and without my examining it. I merely filed it away the same way one would the information that certain cloud types mean rain.

Since my friend had focused my attention on the matter, I have given it extensive time and intensive thought. I have not been content merely to reassociate myself with what I knew, I have examined it from every angle, always asking "why." I have spent many hours on the bottom of trout streams, in holding water, in a plastic mask, seeking additional facts that would further explain why it was holding water.

There were several surprises. One was that some areas which did not appear to be the type which would hold fish when viewed from the surface, actually turned out to be good holding water, containing "hidden assets." Another surprise was that water which from surface examination was labeled holding water was always found to contain fish. This was very gratifying, indicating as it did the thoroughness of my early training and the fact that I had interpreted my early observations correctly—even if not conscious of it at the time.

To the serious angler, learning to identify holding water is of the first importance. It is obvious that all water in a stream cannot contain fish. Therefore, to avoid spending many of his precious angling hours flogging a dead horse, the angler must learn discernment.

It is far easier, it seems, to teach a younger person how to quickly identify holding water than it is to teach his elders. A lad of seven or upwards seems more closely in tune with nature than older people. However, it is something that can be learned, though it comes hard for some.

I know men who are very successful anglers who possess not a whit of streamcraft. They are hard working and persistent and catch fish simply by covering every inch of water which appears

A fast, shallow riffle. There is neither depth nor cover here.

A deep run coming under a bridge. An eleven-pound brown was taken here, September 1967, on a dry fly.

capable of holding a trout. As a matter of fact, most anglers are like this.

I know some, too, who can identify holding water on sight, instantly and correctly. None of these persons were aware of this talent until I mentioned it to them, and like me, when first asked, were unable to say how they had learned or what enabled them to make such identification.

I know one veteran angler, a veritable Edward R. Hewitt, who can not only identify holding water at a glance, but with complete confidence can estimate the size of any fish it may hold. He is more often right than wrong, and I have never known him to be far off in estimating the weight of a fish he has never seen, laying his estimate on the type of hold only.

To go back to my definition of holding water, it must contain at least one of three things: cover, depth, or a broken surface. Frequently all three are present, and in effect all are variations of the same thing—that is, shelter or protection against being seen *from above.*

There is one exception to this; there may be others. In clear streams, in quiet water, trout will sometimes hold at a depth at which they can readily be seen from the surface. Usually these are pools of over five feet in depth; I have discovered trout in very clear, still pools at a depth of ten feet or more.

Usually, in these places there is little bottom cover; this is particularly true of many California streams. It must be that some peculiarity of the fishs' eyesight prevents its seeing "out" from such depths and therefore the fish assumes it cannot be seen from above. Trout in such places do not seem as wary as they do in lesser depths, and though I have never seen them actively feeding in these lies, it is possible to take trout, and good trout, from these deepwater pools.

A rapid pounding into a deep run. Food is constantly brought to the fish by the action of the rapid.

In learning to identify holding water, then, let us ignore the exception. We shall look at first the more easily recognized holds. Perhaps the easiest to spot are drifts, where a log or tree has fallen into an area of good current flow. Other debris has lodged against the original barrier, the current has washed out a hole beneath the pile. Such a place is ideal for trout. It has depth, overhead cover, and a good current flow to carry food back into the trout's lie.

There used to be such a place on the Firehole River. Three

great logs had fallen athwart the stream, smaller branches, sticks and bark had filled the crevices, making a good "roof" over the stream. It was located at the outside of an elbow bend, the current pushed against it with full strength. The entrance of a deep, attractive hole could just be seen under the first log.

I lost two or three dozen wet flies and nymphs in this spot. Some became hooked in the mess, and had to be broken off. The largest number were lost when taken by strong fish, which took refuge among the logs and limbs and could not be forced out. At least, not with my tackle.

One morning, I went down to have just "one more try" at this hopeless case. (Is any case ever hopeless to an angler?) When I arrived, I found I was too late. A rugged old farmer from Minnesota had preceded me and was just leaving. He had three trout totaling just under 14 pounds.

His tackle consisted of a short steel rod, multiplying reel, 25-pound test line, and nylon leader of at least 12 pound test.

"I knew dere vould be big trouts under dere," he told me. "Minute I seen it, I say to myself, 'Yulius, dats de place,' and by yiminy, it vas!!"

He had let the current carry his worm (the stream has since been closed to all but fly fishing) back under the drift, waited patiently for the trout to swallow it, and in his own words, "horsed him out ov dare."

The important thing here is not the strength of the old man's tackle, but the fact he had recognized instantly that "dere vould be big trouts under dere." Uninitiated in the art of trout fishing, he still knew prime holding water on sight.

Subsequently, I saw him at various times along the stream, always fishing spots similar to the one where I met him, and always he had good fish. I've often wondered since if he wasn't doing good work—removing big rusty, old cannibal fish from the stream.

Other types of holding water easily spotted are holes eroded under tree roots, deeply undermined banks, and jumbles of large rocks in the stream bed. While easily spotted, they are not easily fished. Tree roots, especially, are the very devil. I've lost flies and my temper innumerable times fishing such lies. Yet it is well worth the effort to fish these root-guarded lairs; invariably they are the homes of solid old trout.

A fast, rock-filled run downstream from a dropover. Good hot-weather holding spot.

Undercut banks on the outside of curves are one of my favorite forms of holding water. I like to float a dry fly down against the bank a number of times, timing the float, then change to a wet or nymph and repeat the float, giving a little additional time and slack to allow the lure to drift well back in the hole. Usually the strike will come at once, when the lure has reached the innermost recesses of the lie. When the strike does not come at once, it is sometimes advisable to let the fly linger in the area a while, if it will do so. If the current sweeps the fly out and downstream, several more floats into the area are in order.

I am particularly fond of fishing those short, fast, narrow runs caused by an obstruction in the stream—the kind where the current is squeezed between two rocks, or between a rock or log, and the bank. These cause a semi-damming effect. The water increases in depth slightly in front of the obstruction, then pours over or around with increased speed. The force of the current exerts a digging action on the area immediately below, and the water here will be deeper than the water just above, below, or to either side. The bowl-shaped depression formed by current action will be surrounded on all sides by the full flowing rush of the stream, but

A deep, boulder-filled run hosting large trout.

the water in the depression itself will be barely moving; thus it is an ideal place for trout to lie, watching the passing stream for food.

There are many just such areas in the Madison River in the Park. One in particular has never failed to yield at least one two pound trout to a properly presented wet fly. Another contains trout of up to five pounds weight. I have caught several two- and three-pounders from this stretch and have been broken more times than I care to admit.

A shelving ledge pushes out from the right bank about 15 feet. Further out and a few feet downstream a big jagged rock pokes up almost to the surface. From the shallow side on the left bank the whole stream bottom tips or slants toward the right bank. The current at the head of the stretch comes along the left bank, a secondary current follows along the right bank. The slant of the stream bottom from left to right bank causes the main current to slide over and mingle with the right bank current just above the jagged rock.

The combined currents are powerful and move at good speed. The hole below the rock is perhaps five feet deep, shallowing abruptly to ankle-depth on the right, and much more slowly on the left. The depth of the hold continues for perhaps 40 feet, gradually shallowing to knee deep about 100 feet below. The entire surface area is broken.

I have watched scores of people fish this "hole," as it is called locally. All of them, without exception, fished it from the shallow side, and few of them caught other than an occasional whitefish.

The sliding of the current from the shallow to the deep side is responsible. In effect, the fly, although appearing to be presented across and downstream, is presented almost directly down current. It slides over the hole or depression at midwater or higher and is not seen by the fish until it reaches the tail of the stretch, where the whitefish and smaller trout lie.

Standing in ankle deep water on the right side, one is within 15 feet of the deepest part of the depression. The fly cast up and across *stream* is actually cast directly *up current*. Therefore the fly goes much deeper. Even this is seldom deep enough to interest the good fish. The upper surface of the stream above the depression moves quite swiftly—much more so than does the water at the bottom of the depression. So the line or leader is caught in the upper current and swept away before the fly can reach the proper depth.

I use weighted flies here, big flies, and well weighted under the body with fuse wire. Six is the very smallest I use, and four the average; I have used flies as large as 1/0 with success. Frankly, the object is to have a fly heavy enough to get to the bottom and big enough to be seen during the short period the fly lingers in the hold. Pattern is less important than size, although dark flies produce better results.

One day Jim Begley, my next door neighbor from Borger, Texas, who fishes with me each fall, was with me when we saw three men fish this hold. The first was a local angler, and he followed the usual practice of standing in the shallows of the left side and fishing a long line across to the deepest part of the hold.

Jim had never fished this area, but had often heard me comment that most anglers fished it from the wrong side and with the wrong flies. So he watched developments rather closely.

The first man was fishing a Black Wooly Worm, number 6, and a Sandy Mite, number 10. He took one trout of a pound or so on the Wooly Worm, and two whitefish on the Mite, all in the tail of the run. This was about average for this method and location.

The second angler used just one fly, the Black Wooly Worm, number 4, 3x long. Wading in deeper than the first angler, who had departed some five minutes ago, he took a two pound rainbow and lost two others in a half hour's fishing. Then he also departed.

The third angler had been waiting patiently, across on the right bank. When the second angler left, he commenced at once to fish the deeper part of the run. His flies were a Montana Nymph, number 4, and an equally large brown nymph, nameless, he said. In about 30 minutes, he had taken five trout, from 1½ to 2¾ pounds.

Dead water. No cover, little food. Pass it by.

"Well," said Jim, as the last man departed, "there's a perfect example of what you've always told me about this hold. But, it looks like I'll have to wait 'til next year to try it myself. Let's go give Hole Number 2 a try." Which we did, and drew a blank.

An important type of holding water is the long glassy or smooth-topped glide, which has a few large rocks scattered throughout its length. These rocks need not thrust above the surface; in fact, most often they do not. At first glance these glides will appear barren. The water is usually less than three feet deep; the bottom, therefore, is visible in most streams. If not actively feeding, the trout will be lying close under the overhang of the larger rocks.

They will be in deep shadow and motionless. The beginner will usually pass these spots with only a glance. Most old timers spare them only a cast or two.

The fish are there, and even when not actively feeding they can most always be induced to take the fly. (When these fish are feeding, they move upstream of, or alongside the rocks, and sway back and forth at midwater. They are readily seen at this time, and are usually easily taken.) The fly must be presented along the bottom, and must move alongside and past the lie of the fish or the base of rock in a natural manner. I have found the up-and-across stream cast with the fly below the line in a pronounced downstream curve best. (In discussing the fishing of holding water, the use of the wet fly only is considered.)

One reason holding water is so seldom recognized by the angler is because the fish are nearly always concealed from him. This, of course, is the very reason that holding water is what it is; the trout is concealed from the angler (human or otherwise) and the angler in most cases is unseen by the trout.

Thus it is proper to suspect, in any water over two feet deep, the existence of trout. If a broken surface, undercut banks, or good sized rocks are present it will be holding water. The less one sees of trout in waters of this depth or deeper, the more one should suspect their presence.

A single good-sized rock in a shallow riffle will usually hold at least one fish. The current will have dug out alongside and below the rock, creating an area of deeper and quieter water in which the fish may lie without undue exertion. There will nearly always be room to wiggle under the rock and out of sight.

Such holds are a delight to fish, since the precise lie of the fish is known; therefore the most exact and accurate presentation of the fly can be made. Here one will usually find the choice of size and pattern most important. In the West, such water bespeaks the stone or caddis fly nymph, less often the mayfly. My choice for such fishing is usually a size 8 cased caddis imitation, slightly weighted.

A nest of rocks in a large otherwise uncluttered area of a stream is a good bet to hold one or two fish. If this nest or cluster of rocks is arranged to leave an opening in the center it will be certain to contain fish; it is equally certain that it will be most difficult to fish. This is one type of hold where I sometimes revert to the

Hanging ledges and weed beds provide cover in this stretch. Trout run to large size, but are difficult to catch.

dry fly and the "pounding 'em up" or "artificial hatch" methods.

The most difficult kind of holding water to identify is the long, medium-deep run with smooth surface and apparently uncluttered bottom—but a bottom nevertheless—that offers cover to the trout. The angler cannot see the cover and he therefore dismisses the water as barren.

What can offer concealment without itself being visible or noticeable? I refer to those bottoms with longitudinal cracks, crevices, or grooves in them. On a dark bottom these show up only as slightly darker areas and in many cases are less than six inches deep.* A trout may lie in them, his dark-colored back level with and blending into the surrounding bottom; and unless he moves suddenly he will not be seen from above. As a matter of fact, a trout may lie perfectly motionless above a bed of small gravel, in relatively shallow, smooth water and not be seen. His spots blend perfectly with the light and dark pattern of the gravel.

This trout-camouflage is one more example of nature's protective coloring; however the trout does not trust it implicitly. He will believe himself unseen only as long as *you* make no sudden

---

*Six inches deeper than the surrounding bottom.

movement. Fast movement to a trout spells discovery and attack and he flees at once to take cover. Remember this when angling for trout feeding in open water. A slow, smooth movement will not, usually, frighten the fish; a fast jerky movement will.

It took me years to discover the grooved bottom holding water bit. In 1948, while fishing the Firehole River, I found the fish inactive on this stream, which I consider the best dry fly stream in America. After looking in on a half-dozen favored sections and seeing no rises, I took a seat on the bank to rest and watch.

My seat was chosen along a long straight stretch. There was a tree near the bank edge to lean against, in a position which allowed me maximum view both up and down stream. The bottom of the stream in front of me was what I would call conformal. It was shallow near the bank on both sides and sloped evenly to a depth of about three feet in the center. It was nearly smooth, an occasional stick or small stone could be seen but that was all.

I sat there for an hour or so, looking for rises and seeing none. Then, as I turned my head to glance upstream, I suddenly stopped. A movement out in mid-stream caught my eye. As I watched, three shadowy forms rose *out* of the bottom and became three sizeable trout. As the fish moved off slowly upstream—in formation, like a trio of fighter aircraft—I stared hard at the spot from which they had appeared. All I could see was a long narrow streak of what appeared to be slightly darker bottom.

A glance upstream showed that my trio of fish had fanned out and had assumed feeding positions in the stream. Study was forgotten for the moment, as I moved up and dropped a size 16 Adams above the nose of the nearest fish. He took it with a bang, and the ensuing fight scattered the others. After landing the trout (two pounds, two ounces) I went back downstream and waded out to where I had first seen him and his convoy.

In the center of the stream, a long crack or crevice about six inches wide and eight or ten inches deep stretched for 20 feet or so along the bottom. It was smooth sided and as straight as an axe cut. How it came into being is a matter of complete puzzlement; however later study showed that this stream had scores of these bottom cracks. Since that time, I have found such cracks in many streams where there are stretches of bedrock forming the bottom.

Frequently, streams have stretches of holding water that afford

A deep, gliding run. Cover is beneath deeply undercut banks.

cover in the form of underwater "shelves." I do not know what else to call these underwater hideaways. They are almost always found in streams where portions of the bottom is formed of lava. When this molten material was deposited, it formed layers and folds. Quite often some of the layers are of softer material than the layer above or below. When a stream cuts through old lava beds, the softer material is eroded away, and a hanging shelf is left. On first examination, the bottom will appear to have jagged ledges lacing through it; when one wades, his feet to all appearances are on the bottom. In fact, however, the wader is walking on a "shelf" or false bottom, a slab of conglomerate of varying thickness, which is suspended anywhere from several inches to two feet above the true bottom. I have seen such shelves under which could be found spaces that were two feet high and perhaps 10 to 15 feet in length and width. In most cases, the whole thing appears to be a solid ledge, with a dropoff on one or more sides. Seldom can one see back under the edge of the shelf far enough to suspect there is space there. Only by getting down into the water, eyes level with the opening, can one see into this trout hideout; and even then, because it is quite dark, one can only guess at the size of the area. Once, on the Madison, I explored one of

these places with a strong light and face mask and discovered
several trout weighing over five pounds, the existence of which
I was completely unaware before the exploration.

These shelved areas are hard to fish. Even when proper position and weighting allows the fly to get deep enough, a strike is
seldom forthcoming. My explorations were not extensive enough
to supply the complete answer, but I suspect that these trout are
night feeders for the most part. At least, the only successes I have
had in these areas was by late afternoon dry fly fishing. By late
afternoon, I mean after sunset but before the onset of darkness.

A stream with adequate food supply and which has a number
of good holding areas cannot be "fished out." There will always
be a seed stock left no matter how heavy the fishing pressure.
However, there are very many trout streams in the United States
that have adequate food supply but very little holding water.
Such streams become "fished out" early in the season. I know of
several streams on the western slope of the Sierra Nevada where
one will not find a single area of holding water in a mile of stream.
These are fast, shallow, snow-fed streams, subject to heavy runoff in the early spring. By mid-June they have shrunk into a narrow,

*A deep hold, formed by a drift and a curve. Very clear and hard to fish but
worth the effort.*

A fast, heavy run, deeper than it looks. There are very large trout here. This is where my underwater experiments were done.

shallow channel that tumbles precipitously down the mountain.

What few holding areas there are in these streams are usually deep pools at the foot of a fall or a long stretch of rapids. The fish are concentrated here, and so is the fishing pressure. By mid-season, few if any trout are left—certainly not enough to repropagate the stream. Thus, fishing in such streams is a put-and-take affair. One wonders if stream improvement to increase the number of holding areas might be less costly and provide better fishing than the restocking method.

One of the best of the holding water types, especially in terms of larger fish, is the medium deep, weed filled stretch. Here is a trout hotel of the finest quality, abounding in food, with a cover that extends almost to the surface.

Some say that these weedy stretches become too warm for trout. It is true that the temperature in a long weedy stretch will be somewhat warmer than the average. I for one do not believe that trout are especially concerned with water of somewhat more than average warmth, if the water is amply supplied with oxygen. It is my firm opinion that trout grow larger in warmer, well-oxygenated water than they do in equally well oxygenated water of much cooler temperature. For purposes of clarification, I consider water over 75 degrees F. a bit warm and water under 55 degrees F. a bit cool for best trout growth; if the warmer water is very well oxygenated, the fish will feed better and more often than they will in water of, say, 60 degrees or cooler. The reason, of course, is basic: at 75 degrees the trout's digestive system operates faster than at temperatures of 60 degrees or less.

Since green water plants give off considerable amounts of oxygen in the process of growth (and take in carbon dioxide), it follows that weedy waters are better oxygenated than like stretches of the same stream that contain no weeds.

Therefore weed beds, which are one of the best sources of food and cover—those two necessities of life for trout—are by these very factors good holding areas. In some streams, the amount and size of trout found in these weedy stretches exceed those in any other comparable area of the stream.

Good examples of such streams are Silver Creek in Idaho, the upper Owens River in California, Hot Creek and Rising River of the same state, the Firehole River in Yellowstone Park, and many similar streams. It is interesting to note that all of these streams are of higher than average temperature; several of them have hot springs or other hydrothermal sources flowing into them. The uppermost reaches of the Madison River, from its formation by the mingling waters of the Firehole and Gibbon Rivers to about ten miles below, is almost continuously weedy. Once the temperature (which it inherits from its coparent, the Firehole) drops, the weeds thin out and eventually disappear. So it may be that warmer water causes weeds, and not the reverse.

In any event, if the water is 30 inches or more deep, and the weeds do not quite reach the surface, here will be found good trout, and in numbers. Taking them is something else again.

The dry fly man may raise the most fish, but his is a self-defeating business; the very tackle needed to raise the fish reduces to almost a nullity his chances of landing any but the smallest of his victims.

For some reason, the answer to which I hope to have some day, insects hatching in weedy waters seem to run on the small side. Thus, one finds himself fishing size 14 to 22 flies and 5X leaders, a most disheartening state of affairs when one thinks of the chances of landing a three-pound fish out of such waters.

A shallow run leading into a feeding riffle. Your fish will run small here.

It can be done. I once took a three pound, nine ounce brown out of such a weedy stretch on the Firehole. The fish took a size 16 Adams on a 4X leader, and for some reason, or perhaps because of the luck that occasionally smiles on drunks and anglers, fought mostly out in the open. I am not sure what emotion prompts me to recount this small success, for the following day, just below this stretch, in water apparently identical, I hooked and lost 18 fish of lesser size.

My friend Joe Johnson cured me of the habit of using flimsy tackle in such waters. Joe is first and foremost a practical fisherman. He uses eight pound test leader almost always, and shifts down to six pound test with great reluctance.

One time Joe took me to a weed-filled pond a ways west of West Yellowstone. "There aren't many fish in the pond," he said, "but they are all big. So use a strong leader and a big fly."

The weeds were right up to the surface, and it was necessary to fish dry. I put on one of Joe's eight-pound test leaders and a size 4 dry fly tied on a 4X long hook. It was at least three inches long, of a deer hair design meant to imitate the adult stone fly.

I don't know what the trout thought it was but a 4½ pound rainbow took it and was duly landed after plowing through half the weeds in the pond.

Nowadays, if I think it necessary to fish on top in such waters, I use the same formula—and now and then it works. Mostly, though, I wade out and cast upstream with a big, weighted wet fly, which I try to drift down the channels in the weeds. I succeed often enough to keep me happy, and get hung up enough to keep me mad. All in all, it comes out about even, and the size of the fish makes it all worthwhile.

Feeding water, those areas of the stream into which a trout moves only when actively feeding, is present in quantity in nearly every trout stream. Where cover or holding water is some distance away, the trout tend to become night feeders. Night-feeding trout are less wary than day feeders, so they are more easily caught and thus removed from the stream. This fact is responsible for the laws in some states that restrict trout fishing to daylight hours only. These laws attempt to limit the catch by protecting the fish during periods when they lose much of their natural caution.

Feeding water areas are so widely different in appearance that it is hardly possible to describe them, or to separate water into

This glassy-smooth stretch has excellent holds in the form of sunken weed beds. The trout are apt to be anywhere in the area, making fishing to rising fish the only safe method.

feeding and non-feeding areas. In general, deep pools are not feeding water, since underwater insect life in such areas is not usually abundant enough. However, there are many exceptions to this, so it is never safe to label water as non-feeding water just on appearance.

The saving factors of feeding water are that the trout will not be in them unless actively feeding and that usually, if feeding, they can be readily seen, if the approaching angler does not himself frighten them. It does not require a "hatch" of insects in order for trout to move into these feeding areas. However, when trout move into feeding water in numbers, some underwater insect activity is usually responsible.

In any event, when trout are in feeding water, they are there for one purpose—to feed. Since cover is virtually nonexistent, daylight feeding trout will feed very actively while in feeding water, in order to get back to cover or holding water as soon as possible.

Several types of feeding activity will be evident according to the water types. In the swift, shallow riffles, the trout will be "grubbing" or "tailing"—that is, they will be nose down among the rocks and gravel, rooting out nymphs. Now and then a trout will whirl several feet downstream in pursuit of a nymph which has been uprooted and which the current has swept away.

In deeper, slower riffles, the same type of activity takes place, but at a less-hurried pace. The trout cruise around over the bottom leisurely, pausing here and there to pluck some hapless insect from its lair.

Tree roots and drifts. Very good holds for trout, most difficult to fish.

In long, fast runs, the smaller trout will be at the tail of the run, taking leftovers grubbed out by larger trout above. In short runs, the reverse is true. The smaller trout will be at the head of the run, the larger trout at the tail. When insects are missed by the smaller trout, they do not chase them downstream, because just a short distance below, the large trout lie in wait, and the smaller trout would himself be eaten. This applies to runs of such length, depth, and current flow that an insect grubbed loose at the head of the run would be swept to the lower end before finding a new purchase on the bottom.

Trout will often lie in numbers at the foot of a pounding rapid or fall. Here food swept away by the rush and push of the faster current is brought to them all the time. If depth and cover are present, this will be first-class holding water. If cover and depth are not present, trout will "mill" or circle through the area occasionally by day, and flock to the place at night.

There is little need to belabor descriptions of feeding water. Feeding trout in such areas will normally be plainly visible and a moment's observation will enable the observer to determine whether or not they are actively feeding. Usually they will be; otherwise they would not be in such places.

[3]

The Wet Fly and Its Usage

In a lifetime of trout fishing, I suppose I have gone through all the phases a fisherman can go through. I've had wet-fly-only years, dry fly years, spinner, live bait, barbless hook years; and there have been some years when I almost gave up completely. But the older I got and the more I fished, the less I tended to phases, and the more to giving the fish what they seemed to want.

Surprisingly enough, I began to find that bait, hardware, and dry flies were largely unnecessary—or should I say necessary only on special occasions. In the last few years, I've come to the conclusion that 90 percent of trout fishing calls for the wet fly. By "wet fly" I mean all flies fished below the surface, whether they be called nymphs, streamers, bucktails, downwing, upwing, or whatever.

Nowdays I do not use bait or spinner. The difficulty of keeping the one and casting the other to my mind outweighs their usefulness. I use dry flies only when trout are rising or, rarely, just to see them float.

To him who cries bias, I say, not so. I will stake all the fishing tackle I own—and it is considerable—that fishing wet flies day in, day out, on any given stretch of any *clear* trout stream, I will have better fishing than any live bait, spinner or dry fly fisherman, and just as good fishing as anyone who uses all those methods.

I disagree somewhat with those who say pattern is not important. I have fished some hundreds of patterns many thousands of hours, with results that indicate most of them were marginal or occasional producers. I long ago quit using such flies; although

I carry over a hundred patterns in my wet fly book, I use not more than twenty with any regularity and not more than ten steadily. None of these are the so-called "attractor" flies. All the wets I use with any consistency are pretty dull-looking specimens.

The conventional wet fly has been an item of controversy among trout fishermen practically from the moment it came into use. The question of what it resembles or imitates has not yet been settled, nor is it ever likely to be.

Good, I say; this is a healthy and happy situation. It means the more studious among us are going to keep digging to find further evidence to prove our point, and that the wet fly and its use will never become a standardized, hackneyed thing. Thus, we will always be gaining more and more knowledge of our subject, but will never be faced with the fact that this or that theory is inevitably so. Therefore, the least informed among us can deign to argue with the most expert, secure in the knowledge he cannot be shot out of the saddle with incontrovertible facts.

The largest body of wet fly users who seem to agree on one point are those who consider the wet fly to represent a drowned insect. Another group insists the wet fly represents the mature nymph about to hatch. Still another group believes that neither of these is the correct theory and that the trout takes the wet fly out of curiosity. And one very small, very studious and learned group believes the wet fly to represent an adult fly returning to the bottom to lay its eggs. Then all of the above have splinter groups, plus a few indifferent chaps who care less about what the fish think the wet fly represents. This makes for a glorious uproar and keeps the subject eternally alive.

As a confirmed wet fly man, I can't agree completely with any of the above groups, nor can I completely disagree with any of them. And if that isn't a vague, evasive statement, I'll put in with you. My feelings are that all of the above groups are partially right part of the time. I don't believe anybody does know or ever will know what a trout has on his mind when he takes a wet fly, and until we get a trout to talk, one man's opinion seems to be as valid as another's.

I do not have any better theories now about why trout take wet flies than I did over thirty years ago when I first started using them. But I do have some strong reasons for believing the conventional downwing wet fly is not as effective as some more natural appearing flies. As a matter of fact, though I love to tie and like the appearance of the downwing wet fly, I have been reluctantly forced to the conclusion that such flies are not really effective in taking larger trout.

I still make downwing wets, and in my fly book of the 800 to 1,000 flies in the envelopes, a large percentage are of the downwing patterns. But they are there out of habit and because of human love of tradition. I seldom use them, and usually give most of them away during the season.

Ninety-five percent of my wet fly fishing is done with six patterns, none of which resemble the downwing type of fly. These patterns are the Assam Dragon, Montana Stone Nymph and adult, Black Crawler, Skunk Hair Caddis, and Wooly Worm. The Skunk Hair Caddis, and the two stone imitations are fairly good copies of the insect they are supposed to represent. The other three are impressionistic at best, but are among the surest bets to produce good fish. Why, I just don't know, but they are the most consistent producers in my book. There is a general buggy look to all three, and they all appear the same underwater when viewed from any angle. This, I believe, along with their large

Fast, boulder-lined runs on a mountain stream, good wet-fly water.

size, accounts for their success. They are all flies for heavy water, incidentally.

Actually, the Assam Dragon evolved from long study and use of the Fledermouse fly. This is a very successful fly in the west and there are a number of theories as to what it represents. I first thought it represented the gammarus or so-called fresh water shrimp. However, the fly worked very well in streams that did not contain this species. Finally, I decided it was representative of the dragon fly species, whose wide bodied nymph is present nearly everywhere. I may be wrong, of course, but based on that theory, I developed a browner, flatter, heavier fly which has proven very successful for me, even though it does not actually look anything like a dragon fly nymph.

I've used the wooly worm since 1930; it was one of the first patterns I ever tied and used. I had never heard of this fly when I first tied it, and fondly imagined I had originated it. I first tied and fished it as a dry, until by accident I learned how effective it was sunken.

In wet fly usage, as in pattern, I prefer the more natural delivery and presentations. Day in, day out, I catch more and larger fish on the old reliable presentation, which Ray Bergman so aptly calls the "natural drift."

The wet fly presentation is, of necessity, a three-dimensional affair, as opposed to the planar presentation of the dry fly. In heavy current flow, or beneath a broken or discolored surface, the angler is also fishing by "feel." These factors make wet fly presentation far more demanding than dry fly presentation, and refute the dry fly man's gibe that wet fly fishing is a chuck-it-and-chance-it method.

One other factor bedevils the wet fly man: the current flow at the surface is swifter than at mid-water and the mid-water current is swifter than that at the bottom. The wet fly angler, then, not only has to contend with the varying currents from bank to bank, but those between top and bottom as well. Natural presentation of the wet fly thus becomes an extremely complex affair, success in the solving of which can be measured by the catch. Just as the successful dry fly man, the wet fly fisher must present his fly as though it were completely detached before success is his. As to which is the more demanding art, an internationally famous angler once said, "I can name any number of good dry fly men, but I can count the good wet fly men I know on the fingers of one hand."

In fishing the natural drift, I find there are—here in the West at least—many excellent lies that cannot be successfully fished without using weighted flies. The man who says otherwise is badly misinformed or inexperienced. I remember an angler—and a very good one too—who always turned up his nose at using any kind of weight. He could fish any lie in any stream, he said, without weight, just by selecting the proper places to stand and cast. He held this belief until I fished down a heavy run behind him one day. He caught two small trout and a host of whitefish. I caught four, all of which weighed nearly two pounds.

After a comparison of flies and techniques, my friend, an Eastern angler, agreed to try the next run as a test. He was convinced when I took two good trout out of small pockets where no combination of stance and cast would allow the proper settling of his unweighted fly.

My friend still does not and will not use weight. He prefers to fish those areas where his unweighted flies will do the job, and since there are plenty of streams containing such holding areas, he makes out well enough.

There are times when I almost agree with him. When a strong following wind lays hold of my weighted fly and slams me in the back or neck with it, I am tempted to give them up. But I am lazy, and I dearly love to fish heavy water, so I bear with their poor casting qualities and continue to use them.

I am convinced that the only place to take large fish, when no insect activity (prehatch) is evident, is on the bottom. I waste no time fishing at midwater, and none near the surface unless flies are hatching.

Therefore, wet fly fishing to me means getting the fly down to the bottom where the fish can see it. This is why I use weighted flies and why I invariably cast upstream.

In order to have the fly drift naturally and get down well too, it is often necessary to have some amount of slack between rod and fly. I have heard anglers say otherwise, but I remain unconvinced. It is true that many strikes will be missed when fishing in this manner, but I, for one, would rather miss a strike than not to receive a strike at all.

For several years I fished with a young fellow who was of the "no slack" school. He used weighted flies, even as I, and at the end of the day, we usually found our catch about the same. This proved, said the young angler, that my method was all wet. Certainly it appeared little more effective than his taut line method but it was more fun, for I was getting strikes every few minutes while my friend sometimes went hours between them. And on most days, the largest fish caught fell to my slack line drift.

There were other factors here, too, that affected the outcome. My young friend fished almost every day throughout the season; I was able to fish only an occasional weekend and during vacation. The younger fellow had the benefit of more practice, which helped develop his "touch" or "feel," and also the sharper reflexes of youth. He therefore hooked a larger percentage of the fish that struck than I could have, had I fished his method. On the other hand, when he tried my method, he got far more strikes; but upon missing one or two, he would become disgusted and revert to his taut line fishing. In the long run, he became convinced that the natural drift did produce more strikes and, in general, larger fish. But he never acquired the patience to use the method.

Similarly, I never was able to develop an interest in fishing the deeper, still pools. Casting the fly out, waiting for it to sink, and slowly retrieving it seems like a dull business to me, although the method does produce good trout and in lakes is just about the only consistent wet fly method. If you assume I do not fish lakes much, you would be right.

It takes more skill than is at first apparent to successfully fish still waters. The cast must not be bungled, the pickup must not rip the water. The above-water portion of the line must be watched like a hawk while the fly is sinking, and the retrieve must not be too fast. Any defection is readily seen by the trout in such waters and usually spells finish to one's chances in that pool for that day.

It is a reliable, though slow, method of taking larger trout. For those who excel in its practice, it is very rewarding. However these chaps are scarce in this country, although I am informed this is a common method in England and Europe, and that people become skillful indeed in this form of presentation.

When I turned away from conventional wet fly design and began to tie what I thought were more natural appearing patterns, I made them with flattened bodies and lighter colored bellies. Much to my disappointment, these flies were utter failures.

There had to be a reason for such failure, and since I had had such high hopes for my new designs, I set out rather grimly to find out why they didn't work.

At first I was stymied. Nothing I could dig up gave me the slightest clue. I might have never known the reason for fish refusing these flies if I hadn't bought a plastic face mask for entertaining the kids of a house-guest. Exploring the bottom of the swimming pool with these youngsters, I found enough nickels and dimes to keep them in pop and ice cream. It didn't take long for the light to dawn. Here was a way of checking up on my failures, and perhaps of finding out why they were failures, and more besides.

I won't go into the difficulties of spying on trout and trout flies. I quickly learned that a trout stream is not a swimming pool. But the difficulties were not insurmountable, and I did get my answers.

The culprit, quickly found, was the one that has bedeviled the dry fly man forever—to wit, the leader. As the wet fly moved along, the currents above the fly plucked and pulled at the leader, turning and twisting it, and the fly followed along, willy nilly, showing its back, belly, and all sides. Now, any wet fly behaved this way; but on flies that were unflattened, and lacked contrasting body colors, it was difficult to see that the fly twisted and turned.

Real, live insects in trout streams do not twist and turn—vertically, that is—when caught by the current. They may be spun around and round, thrust here and there, but their backs remain uppermost, and their bellies cannot be seen—except when they move toward the surface to hatch.

Among the patterns used in this experiment was the wooly worm, and it seems that one reason this fly is so effective is because it always looks the same from any angle. Therefore, it appears to be in control of its actions, so it appears alive.

Also easily noted when down on the bottom of a trout stream were the times when the fly did not move at the same speed as the surrounding water. When the fly and current moved at the same speed, the fly "bloomed"; its fur, hackles, etc., flared out and looked very lifelike. When the fly moved faster than the current, its fur, hackles, etc. were compressed, and the fly also assumed unlifelike positions. When the fly moved slower than the current, the fly reversed and appeared very unnatural.

There were fish in the stretch where this experiment was performed, and their actions were very enlightening. When any object, stick, leaf, fly or whatever, appeared within the trout's range of vision, the fish turned toward it. As soon as the object was recognized as non-edible, the fish lost interest, except in some cases where small sticks and bits of grass or reed were taken into the fishes' mouth in a testing manner, then ejected. Some small bits of stick might be taken in and ejected two or three times.

When a fly appeared, the fish showed instant interest. But if the fly were twisting or turning, or behaving in a decidedly unnatural manner, the fish lost interest at once. It was plain to me, and obviously to the fish also, that in a fly with contrasting back and belly colors it was easier to detect unnatural motion.

Now and then, when a fly of normal tie (as opposed to the dark back light belly type) acted somewhat unnaturally, the fish would move up to it, then drift along with it, inspecting it closely. Often, during such performances, the trout would actually touch the fly with its nose. Sometimes, after following the fly for several feet, the fish would take it; but this was not usual.

When the fly appeared to act quite naturally, the fish would usually move forward and take it immediately, unless, in the period between spotting and taking, the fly made some unnatural movement. When this happened the trout immediately became wary. Sometimes the fly made an unnatural movement just as the fish was about to take it. This caused the trout to flare wildly away, and usually he stayed away.

The more naturally the fly acted, the more naturally the fish took. One thing that was quite evident: when the fish hit hard, it was either because there was more than one fish after the same fly, or else, a quick, but natural movement of the fly, just as the fish was about to take, caused the fish to think his lunch was trying to escape. I had had many sharp, smashing strikes in this area, and I now know that most of these were caused because of competition for the fly.

In Alaska, I had spent many days watching fish take or refuse the fly in the Clearwater, one of the most aptly named of streams. I thought I had learned a lot, but until getting down to the fishes' level, I really was quite uninformed on the taking techniques of wet fly angling.

From the outset, it could be plainly seen that no fish were badly frightened by the fly, no matter how unnaturally the fly acted. But if the pickup was made while fly and leader were in the vicinity

This run is the finest wet-fly (nymph) water I know. It consistently produces two- to four-pound fish. Large boulders and the broken surface provide shelter and cover.

of a fish, that fish promptly sought cover and stayed there for some time. The very important thing to be learned here is not to pick up the fly while it or the leader is still within the area of the hold.

This experiment was used to observe the difference in action between weighted and unweighted flies. Not only did we learn that the weighted flies floated deeper and more naturally, but also that trout in holding water seldom look up. Flies, sticks, reeds, etc. which drifted by on or below the fishes' level were inspected, and either taken or rejected. The same type of objects drifting along more than a few inches above the fishes' level were entirely ignored. I can only assume that the fish simply did not see them.

The most taking method, without any doubt, was to cast up and across current, well above the expected lie of the fish, and make the cast so that the fly landed well down current of the line. In essence, this was exactly like the dry fly angler's curve cast, but much exaggerated. The best casts were those in which the line landed cross current at least ten feet above the fly.

Even when well executed, this cast did not always result in a good float. Sometimes contrary upper currents would seize the line or leader, or both, and twitch and twirl the fly, thus spoiling the whole effort. Sometimes 20 to 30 casts were necessary to produce one good drift. Sometimes the drift would be perfect, but the attention of the fish would be elsewhere until the fly had passed his lie. However, when the drift was good, and the fly was seen by the fish, the take was strong and sure.

We used a total of seven hook sizes, fourteen patterns, and three color variations of one pattern in this experiment. Hook sizes 12, 10, 8, 6, 4, 2 and 2/0 were used. The patterns were the wooly worm (black, olive green, and yellow), Assam Dragon, a two-toned nymph, Professor, Quill Gordon, Leadwing Coachman, California Stone Fly, Montana Nymph (black), Vint's Special, Skunk Hair Caddis, Sandy Mite, Black Gnat, Whirling Dun, and White Miller. Only four flies—the White Miller, Sandy Mite, the two toned nymph, and Professor—did not catch fish.

The reasons for the failure of these four flies, to one down on the stream bottom, appeared obvious. The Sandy Mite, in sizes 10 and 12, simply never got down within two feet of the fishes' level. The White Miller, although it drifted time and again at the proper level, and appeared, on several drifts, to act quite naturally, never once interested the fish. The Professor drew several indications of interest, but all the trout broke off their inspection before approaching closer than 12 inches. It was apparent that the fly somehow lacked appeal. The two-toned nymph will be dealt with later.

All three colors of the wooly worm brought strikes. This fly, the Assam Dragon, and the Montana Nymph were about equal in producing strikes, and topped all others. On the basis of the limited time spent on the experiment, the other eight patterns seemed about equal to each other in the number of strikes produced.

The two-toned nymph, which I had previously pinned my hopes upon, and the failure of which led to this experiment, not only failed to produce a strike, but it also produced a reaction from the fish which I can only describe as shocked surprise. Because of its dark back and light belly, every twist, turn, and roll made by the fly was quite clearly seen. No matter how many times it was drifted through the hold, it never once failed to signal that it was a fraud by alternately exposing its back and belly.

I later tried this fly in quiet water where more control over the drift could be maintained, but, while it did produce fish, it was no better than several other patterns and I finally discarded it completely.

My little underwater experiment was well worth the time spent, and resulted in the biggest single step forward in my entire angling career. No longer do I desert a good hold or lie until certain the fish therein have had the opportunity to see my fly, and see it behaving naturally. To achieve a natural appearance from nearly every angle, I've tended toward the use of flies which appear the same when viewed from any direction.

Now for the hook sizes. I became convinced during this experiment that hook, or rather fly, size was of great importance. The larger fish plainly showed preference for larger sizes, although not the very largest. Incidentally, the results for the sizes 10 and 12, and the 2 and 2/0 were about equal; but these sizes were less effective than those hooks in the middle of the range used. The reasons for the sizes at the upper and lower ends of the scale not being so effective as the others were not the same for both ends of the range.

The smaller flies were more often missed by the fish—that is, not seen. On the other hand, the larger sizes were seen by the fish on nearly every drift, but, although they evoked some attention, it seemed that the fraud was too easily detected.

Based on my stream bottom observations, it appeared that a fish must see color in much the same way as a human. The colors most readily visible to me also appeared to be most quickly noticed by the trout. Colors that showed the most contrast with the stream bottom were most quickly seen by me, and I believe by the fish also. Dark colors were most easily detected; black was tops. The White Miller was also highly visible. Medium colors were sometimes hard to see against the stream bed, which by some odd optical illusion appeared bowl-shaped.

During the tests, some twitching retrieves were tried, but the trout did not show the slightest interest in flies used in this manner.

Incidentally, we cut the points off the hooks when making this experiment. This proved to be a good idea, for in covering the hold, the line, leader, and sometimes the hook dragged across my body. After I had gotten settled into position in my chosen place, the trout seemed not at all disturbed by my presence as long as I made no sudden moves.

The hold or run in which we made these experiments had a very strong current flow, a maximum depth of between four and five feet, and contained several good-sized boulders. The water temperature at stream bottom ran from 59 to 63 degrees. In order to keep warm, and to better blend with the bottom, I wore woolen pants and shirt, and thermal underwear.

The above experiment confirmed my long-held belief that the most important thing in wet fly fishing is to cover the hold thoroughly. One must use several casts through exactly the same area to make sure that the trout see at least one drift with the fly behaving naturally.

When commencing an assault on a stretch of holding water, make your first casts from the bank, if possible. Cover the area through which you intend to wade, before wading in. Then, when in the first wading position, start casting a rod's length out, and about 15 feet upcurrent.

Make at least three drifts or series of casts, before lengthening line. The next series of several casts or drifts will be about one foot further upcurrent and one foot further out. Keep extending out and up until casting 30 or 35 feet. Then move to a new spot and commence the pattern over. Make certain the cast-drift patterns overlap.

No long casts are made until all the holding area possible has been covered in the manner described. Then attempt to wade to positions that will allow the remaining portions of the hold to be systematically covered. Always, strive for short casts, repeated drifts down the same groove, and complete line control.

This method of water coverage accomplishes several things. It assures that the fly is first drifted through any water where the angler intends to wade. It places the fly up or up and across on every cast. This helps to attain depth on the drift. The short cast gives the best possible chance of good hooking percentages. It virtually guarantees the fish an opportunity to see the fly, no matter what his position. It offers the best opportunity for a natural appearing presentation.

If this method of coverage yields no strikes, repeat the same pattern of casts and drifts, but after the fly reaches the end of its drift, hand retrieve it five to ten feet. On alternate drifts, let the fly drop back once or twice during the retrieve.

It is a bad day when these two methods do not bring several strikes. But it does happen. When it does, stop fishing and find a spot where you can look in on the fish. (See the chapter on "Solving the Problem.") If you get no clue to the answer after 15 to 30 minutes of observation, commence a third series of cast-drifts, lifting and dipping the rod tip throughout the drift. Use the same covering pattern.

The next presentation involves the same type coverage, but the fly is stripped in by hand during the drift. Pulls of six or so inches are used. This system is hard work, because it requires many more casts to cover the same water and both hands are involved.

These four methods are the four basic wet fly presentations. I use them in the order related because experience has shown them to be proportionately effective. The first method produces results a larger percentage of the time than do the other three put together.

I normally use a two fly cast. Some years back I used a three fly cast at times. I do not remember a single instance of taking a fish on the hand fly. When I first noticed this, I was puzzled. After stewing about it one winter, I decided on an experiment.

When using the three fly cast, all three flies were of different patterns. Apparently, I'd been using the wrong pattern on the upper end of the leader. So the next year, when fishing the three fly cast, I used three identical flies. I have yet to catch my first trout on the hand fly. To me this is further proof that the fish want their wet flies on the bottom.

At times, when fish aren't coming normally, experiment with a two fly cast of streamers or bucktails handled in the same manner as the regular wets. Sometimes it works; if it doesn't, 30 minutes of use is enough time to determine this.

When prehatch activity is evident, most any conventional wet fly method will work, but some methods are better than others.

The method that has worked best for me is a two fly cast of unusual makeup. A large bulky fly is used on the tail. This fly is to provide weight and drag, so pattern is not important. The dropper should be a nymph-like fly of the type involved in the prehatch activity.

The cast is made up and across, and allowed to drift naturally the first few feet. Then the line is brought just taut, and the rod raised and lowered. Line should be retrieved only enough to keep it just taut, and the motion of the rod tip should be quite deliberate. About six or eight inches of motion each way is about right.

Some nymphs become very active just prior to hatching. Depending on the type, they will move around on the bottom, drift along just above the bottom, or move toward the surface and back toward the bottom. The appearance is one of nervousness, and the method just described is an attempt to simulate this activity.

The movement of the nymphs excites the fish, which will commence to feed eagerly. If you strike one of these periods and your presentation is convincing, you will be in for one of those red letter days. I have seen cases where this type activity lasted for over three hours.

During such a period, one must be alert for the fish to quit hitting, while insect activity goes on unabated. If this happens, remove the tail fly, and use the natural drift. If this gets no action, use a weighted nymph of the proper type and cast upstream. Leave the dropper fly as is.

Should the above two switches fail to get action, you probably have a bona fide dry fly hatch on your hands, and a switch to the floater is in order. But in most cases, I believe you will do better with one or all of the wet fly methods.

A typical example of this kind of activity comes to mind. I had just arrived on the stream bank (the Madison) about a quarter of a mile above the cable crossing near The Barns. Activity started while I was rigging up.

I put a big weighted fly on the tail and tied on a number 6 Brown May Nymph as a dropper. Using the first method described, I had excellent results for about 30 to 45 minutes. Then I ceased to get strikes, although there was more fish activity than ever.

I took off the tail fly and substituted another unweighted Brown May Nymph for it. Using the natural drift, casting up and across, I stayed busy for another half hour or so, then the fish stopped hitting.

Surface rises were apparent, but I didn't put on the dry fly. Instead, I put on a 7½ foot tapered leader, greased down to within 18 inches of the tip, and tied on a Tups Nymph, size eight.

Drifting this along the surface film, I did smashingly, taking several trout larger than any so far taken. And when the fish quit striking this time, they were through for the day. I didn't much care. In a little over two hours I had landed and released 13 fish weighing from one to two and one-half pounds.

Such events come all too rarely, but one should be prepared to take full advantage of them. Since this type of activity seldom lasts very long, it is a shame to have to waste time experimenting to find the right lure and presentation.

A deep, boulder-lined run; good wet-fly fishing with weighted fly. You must get down to the fish; they will not come up to your fly.

An exciting method of wet fly fishing when conditions are right for its use is one that I call "skimming." The old angler who introduced me to this method called it "skimming the riffles," and I have just shortened his title.

A longer rod works better than a shorter one. I prefer and use an 8½ foot rod for this fishing. A cast of two or three flies is used, spaced about two feet apart. I prefer to use three flies of the same pattern, with color variations. Most anglers, however, use different patterns, with the hand fly matching the emerging natural.

The cast is necessarily short, for good line control is a must with this method. Make the cast directly across. The instant the flies touch, raise the rod and commence a rod and hand retrieve.

An irregular jumpy retrieve works best, and the flies must be kept well up on the surface.

I've had best success with this method in fast, broken riffles, and swift runs not over two feet deep. The method is most deadly when a few flies are hatching. It works better on calm, clear days.

One wet fly method which I don't often use, but which is good under certain precise conditions, involves the use of a dry fly.

Many good trout lie under drifts, undercut banks, and the like, which contain obstacles that entangle or hang up an ordinary wet fly drifted into these spots. Hanging up can be reduced considerably by using a stiffly hackled, fully palmered dry fly. A brown, grizzly, or badger bivisible is good. Plain palmer ties of any subdued color work fine. Just make sure the hackle is the best dry fly quality and quite full and thick. A snagproof fly is what is desired.

Quite often, treating the fly with oil will help, because in certain of these spot lairs, floating food washes up against the upstream edge of the lie, and is sunk by the action of the current. In such cases, the fish will be lying well up and forward, alert for such tidbits. Quite often, the strike will come just as the fly vanishes.

In case the fly isn't taken at once, enough slack should be given to allow the fly to cover the lie. Sometimes even the palmer tied dry fly will hang up in these areas, but a regular tie has no chance at all.

A stout leader is called for. It must be strong enough to offer a fair chance of breaking loose from a root or limb, and it must be strong enough also to haul a three or four pounder bodily from such a lie.

Brute strength isn't all that's required. Once the strike comes, the hook must be sunk home and the fish hustled rapidly out of his abode before he can get set for a tussle. If you don't get him out of there in a hurry, you probably wont get him out at all. These wise old lunkers seem to know all the tricks, and will use them if you give them time.

The wet fly fisherman, to get full benefit from his method, must always be ready to use the presentation that will get his fly to the fish in a natural manner. Any method that will allow this should not be spurned. But, most of the time, the deep natural drift, and thorough coverage of the hold will bring best results. It's the basic method.

[4]

Taking Worthwhile Trout

It was once said, with considerable truth, that the definition of a living wage depended upon whether you were paying it or receiving it. Something of the same is true concerning worthwhile trout. Only in this area there are more than two viewpoints to consider. No definition of the word worthwhile can be made unless the variables of "while" are considered.

For instance, a 10-inch trout in a stream 20 miles away might be considered worthwhile, while a 15-incher that could only be caught after a 200 mile drive might not be. Or in a state not blessed with trout streams, any trout might be considered worthwhile.

I have some friends, whom, many years ago, I taught to tie flies, and thus indirectly introduced them to trout fishing. Each year, they drive some 700 miles to spend a couple of weeks catching six- to twelve-inch trout. I tried to convince them that it would be more worthwhile to drive 2000 miles, and catch one- and two-pounders. They pointed out that this would, round trip, be about three times the distance, take three times as long to drive, and would be more than three times as expensive. We never became reconciled on this point. I would rather make one such trip every three years, but my friends preferred smaller fish every year. We're still friends.

So, the worth of a trout, like beauty, is in the eye, or mind, of the fisherman. For me, I wouldn't drive ten miles to catch 10-inch trout if I could drive a thousand and catch trout weighing over a pound. On the other hand, I wouldn't walk across the road to catch the monsters in Lake Pend Oreille. I simply am not interested in giant trout, or pygmy trout. Just middle-sized ones.

So, everyone must decide for himself what his definition of "worthwhile trout" is. For me, as I've said, it's trout over a pound and up to whatever size strikes while I'm angling. But, it's the over-one-pound fish that my efforts are aimed at.

Being in the same place where worthwhile trout are, or angling exclusively for them, is no guarantee of success. There are scores of fishermen who stand thigh deep in the best trout streams in the nation, season after season, and habitually catch nothing but six- to ten-inch trout.

Trout fishing, like draw poker, is a game of skill, with no luck connected with it. Although some speak of the luck of the draw, in reality there is no such thing. There are percentages connected with the draw, but not luck. In time the percentages favor every-one equally. A man may catch a royal flush the first hand he ever plays, or a five-pound trout the first time he angles for one. But there are so many royal flushes per million hands dealt, and so many five-pound trout per million casts. Winning one hand or catching one five-pound trout is luck. Play a hundred thousand hands, or make as many casts, and the percentages will get you every time. Luck has nothing to do with sustained performance in any field.

Just as a poker player can develop his skill only by playing, so an angler can develop his only by angling. But in either case, practice and experience do not guarantee success.

A poker player who "enjoys a friendly game of poker" will never be a serious threat to the man who plays to win, simply because they have different objectives. One man enjoys the game, but cares little for the pot. The other enjoys raking in the pot. He may also enjoy the game, but not so much that he is willing to pay for the privilege.

I like to play draw poker—to win. When I sit down to a game I announce to one and all that it is my intent to quit as a winner. When I go angling, I go with the serious intention of catching worthwhile fish. At least, most times. Sometimes, I do go fishing just for the fun of it, and usually, that's what I catch.

In order to catch worthwhile fish, a stream containing such fish must be found. When I was younger, I thought one had to get miles off the beaten track. I packed into many such streams only to find them full of small fish. After a while, as I became more adept at reading the water, I realized that, in many cases, the hardest fished streams were the best bet for worthwhile fish. This was because the yearlings and the hatchery trout were caught out and the real good lies were taken by fish too wily for the average angler to catch.

Finding this out didn't result in my suddenly beginning to catch dozens of worthwhile trout. Although I had learned to read the water in order to locate the fish, I still had to learn the flies and methods that would interest such fish.

The biggest step forward in my angling career came because I learned that the insects on which trout feed, exclusive of terrestrials, spent 99 percent of their insect life on the bottom of the stream. Therefore, it followed that a trout would spend the greatest portion of his feeding hours searching the bottom, where the food was.

Knowing this, and being able to do something about it, were different stories. No one has ever solved the problem of getting a wet fly to the bottom of a stream, and having it behave as though it were unattached, with any regularity. Unless the blamed thing *was* unattached, which is not much help.

Weight, either in the fly or on the leader, helps to get the fly down. So do sinking lines. But there still remains the problem of varying current speeds from rod tip to fly, and from top to bottom. The line, leader, and therefore the fly, are affected by all these currents, and with this in mind, one begins to see the complexity of the problem.

There is no simple way to solve that problem. Even when you can read the water expertly, there may be cross currents which you're unable to detect but which nevertheless affect the drift of the fly. About all that you can do is to use your best judgment in getting into position, and try to drop the fly where your experience tells you you're apt to get the best drift.

If you get no action, there are four possibilities as to why not: One, the trout may not be feeding; two, there may be no trout in the lie; three, you may not be quite in the right position; four, your fly may not be deep enough.

Non-feeding trout are of little concern to me. It is my contention that if you present the lure naturally where it is convenient for the trout to take it, he will take it most times, hungry or not.

If there are no trout in the lie, then you are not adept enough at reading and identifying holding water. If several changes of position produce no action, and if you are convinced there *should* be a trout there, chances are your fly is not deep enough. In most trout holds, I want the fly riding deeply enough so that I feel it tick the bottom now and then. Or, as the saying goes, "if you are not getting hung up once in a while, you're not fishing right."

Once you believe that you're in the right position, and the fly is searching the bottom, do not give up and move on without making 30 to 50 drifts through the hold. Then, and only then, is it safe to move on.

The above is predicated on the choice of fly being a reasonable one for the stream and the area being fished. It will do you little good to drift a yellow marabou the size of a turkey through thin clear water holding brown trout. But if your fly is one which can be expected to produce at that time of year on that stream, then persistence is justified and will usually pay off.

What about the fly? Well, what about the natural insects in the stream? How big are they? What are their prevailing color tones? Are they creepers or free swimmers?

Not being too much of a believer in the exact imitation theory, I still think your best chance is with a fly that simulates the natural insect in size, shape, and prevailing color. Also, I'm a firm believer that unless the fish are definitely feeding on a certain type insect a fly representing the largest of the indigenous naturals is the best bet to produce worthwhile trout. In most waters, give me the big stone fly or dragon nymph types as a starter. Actually, a well made, large stone fly nymph is also a good representation of the largest of the mayfly types (Hexagenia). So, these two, dragon fly and stone fly nymph, cover several possibilities, and offer the trout a large mouthful at the same time.

Much as I preach the doctrine of the large fly, I am occasionally caught not practicing what I preach. One September, Jim Begley and his son, Dr. Lew Begley, conned me into a trip into Grebe Lake, which took about as much doing as falling off a log.

Going on the theory that grayling have small mouths, Jim and I were using small flies, number eights. But Lew, knowing nothing about grayling, put on a very large fly. We all started catching fish immediately, but it didn't take long for us to notice that Lew was catching the largest fish by far.

"What on earth are you using there, Lew?" Jim demanded of his son.

"That big purple fly you gave me," replied Lew, meanwhile hauling in another 15-inch grayling.

"Good grief!" said Jim, appalled, "that fly is such a monstrosity that I called it the 'Purple Horror.' Now, look at what he's doing with it."

Jim and I quickly put on large flies, number fours, and right away started catching larger fish; and we came out that day with what the rangers said was the largest average size grayling they had ever seen from Grebe Lake.

The fly that had started us on the right track looked like nothing so much as a purple sausage with a little collar of black hackle. It was a number 4, 5x long, with a body fully as thick as a man's little finger.

The saga of the Purple Horror didn't end here. Lew wanted to take enough fish back to banquet the doctors at the hospital. Next to grayling, our best eating fish are cutthroat, so the three of us went over to the Yellowstone River to lay in a supply.

The fish here ran just about a pound, but they had no difficulty in inhaling the Purple Horror, and Lew outfished the both of us.

"What do you think of that scoundrel?" Jim wailed. "Not only does he outfish his old man but he does it with a fly I gave him."

"Maybe he'll give it back to you," I said.

"Nothing doing," said Lew, shying away. "Pa's been trying to get me to use big flies for years. Now that I've got one that works, nobody is taking it away from me."

"Well, anyway, you can make some more," I told Jim.

"That's the heck of it," he said ruefully. "I don't have any more of that purple material. But, I won't get caught using too small flies again, you can bet." To which I add, amen.

Throughout this book, I am assuming that the reader will be an advanced enough angler to observe fish actively feeding, and to be guided accordingly. I also am assuming that the reader knows that this condition doesn't exist very often. It never seems to exist if we have made a long trip to be on the stream only a short time. "You should have been here yesterday" is a cry that all of us have heard too often.

Nearly all streams hold worthwhile trout, even if most of the fish in the stream are small. In these cases, the angler must concentrate his efforts on those holds which are most apt to be the homes of the larger fish. If the hold is small, and a few casts produce a small fish, you'd be advised to move on. Six-inch trout and sixteen-inch trout seldom occupy the same hold. On the other hand, two or more trout of a similar size will often occupy the same area, so if you catch a decent trout out of a hold, a few additional drifts should be made through the area on the off chance your trout may have had a friend.

Jim Leisenring of Pennsylvania, a noted Eastern wet fly fisherman, and a firm believer in taking worthwhile trout, spent about as much time locating his fish as he did in catching them. He favored the smaller but better holds—the kind which were some distance from other holds, and which were apt to contain just one fish.

After locating the hold, Leisenring would decide on the fly, the method, and the position he deemed best; not until then would he wade in and start casting.

There is no more reliable way to come up with worthwhile trout. It is a shade too methodical for me, however, and possibly for most other anglers. But if I were to set out to make the best showing on any given day, that would be my approach. I do not believe it can be beaten.

This approach lends itself to several methods of presentation. The deeply sunken natural drift is extremely successful, because better line control is usually possible in fishing these small holds than would be possible if a large area were being covered. Also, quite often, the exact depth of the lie can be told, and the fly dropped the correct distance up-current to plumb the depth during the drift.

In some of these areas, the rising-to-the-surface method is fantastically successful. This is true of those areas where the precise lie of the fish is known, and where the currents are not too complicated. A short cast is usually called for, so that the fly can be handled more precisely.

A combination of the two methods has served me best. In this presentation, the position, and the spot to drop the fly, are chosen as though for the natural drift. But as the fly approaches the known, or expected, lie of the fish, the line is brought just taut, and kept that way until the strike comes, or the fly has definitely passed the area of the hold. This method produces a consistently high hooking percentage, and just about as many strikes as any method.

In a heavily fished stream, taking worthwhile trout may call for angling for specific fish. If so, it is to be expected that lies for such worthwhile trout are not too plentiful, and that fishing some of them may not be possible using orthodox methods.

I recall such a lie on the Merced River, near the Arch Rock ranger station. A huge boulder thrust into the stream, and the current slid along the face of the boulder full strength. On the downstream side, another smaller rock hung out over the little eddy formed by the damming action of the larger rock. The eddy beneath the smaller stone was relatively quiet, and just large enough to house one good fish. The fish was there; he could be seen. But it was impossible to drift a fly to him by orthodox methods. The current sweeping by carried the line right along with it, and the fly was snatched by the eddy in an obviously unrealistic manner.

One day when I was checking creels in the area, I decided to go study the spot once more to see if I could figure out a way to catch the big fellow. When I arrived, there was an angler already there, on top of the larger boulder. There was a deep bend in his rod, and the taut line disappeared beneath the lower rock. He had the big one on.

The fish was duly landed and I went up to officially measure the fish, and collect a couple of scales for the lab. The fish went 21 inches, a fine, healthy fish in every respect.

The angler had taken him on a size eight caddis worm imitation. What surprised me was that there was a dipsey sinker weighing at least an ounce strung on the leader. The leader, about nine or ten feet long, was run through the eye of the sinker.

The angler saw me eyeing this rig and hastened to explain. He had been raised and learned to fish in the east, on hard-fished streams. At an early age, he found that many spots holding good trout could not be fished with flies, but that bait could be dunked into these lairs. Being a determined fly fisherman, he had adapted bait fishing methods. In this case he had lowered the rig alongside the rock, and when the sinker hit bottom he released a carefully calculated amount of slack.

The fly then had drifted down current, ahead of the leader, and in a very natural manner. The fish had nailed it hard the instant it came into view. Incidentally, this angler called cased caddis nymphs "periwinkles."

I was somewhat skeptical, but later on had a chance to try the method on the same stream. Here, tall grass had lopped over, and made a tunnel in the water alongside the bank. The tips of the grass had then become caught on the bottom. Thus, the only way to get a fly into the tunnel was from upstream. I had tried this several times but with no success; the line or leader always caught in the grass.

I used the dipsey sinker method, and on the first try hooked an 18-inch rainbow. On two later occasions, I caught a 15- and a 17-incher, both browns, from this spot. It is about the only method for fishing such lies with the fly. It is very good for fishing beneath drifts, or sunken logs.

One of the most sporting and exciting methods, as well as one of the oldest, of fishing the fly has never found much favor in this country. It is possible to use this method only under certain, rare circumstances; but when these circumstances occur, it is about the only feasible method of fishing the fly.

The method is known, in Ireland at least, as *dapping*. In some other countries it is known as skean fishing, waking, skipping, or skittering, to name a few. It is only workable when there is a high wind, and it usually works best when the wind is so high that no other method of fly fishing is feasible.

A long rod, unfinished line, and bushy fly are the best tools for this exciting form of fishing. One stands with his back to the wind, and lets the fly and line be billowed out from the tip of the upright rod. As the line becomes longer and longer, the fly will dip and flutter over the surface, occasionally touching or dapping. It is at this point that the action comes, and spectacular it sometimes is.

I never thought much about this method, dismissing it as impractical, until one Christmas, when my wife got me a grab-bag assortment of items from Herter's. Included was an unfinished fly line.

I had been plagued the preceding fall by high winds in the Madison-Firehole meadow areas. At that time, I had thought about the Irish method of dapping, of which I had read, but had not the right kind of line to try it. Now, I did have, and I admit

I was rather looking forward to it, as I spooled the unfinished line onto a spare reel.

Well, the next time the wind blew, I was ready. It was a picnic. The wind was gusty, but strong; it was blowing hoppers, dragon flies, crane flies, and a few emerging caddis, into the water. The fish were slashing at the skating, skittering insects in a frenzy. When my big, bushy variant started dipping and skipping, the fish flung themselves on it with great abandon. For each fish hooked, several would slash at it, but miss. I would strike lustily at some of the misses. The whole thing was hilarious, but productive, too. I left the stream that evening with a greater feeling of satisfaction than I ever had on any such windy day before.

If you would like to give this exciting game a try, unfinished lines can be had from many of the fly tying material houses for as little as $1.50. Any spare reel, your regular rod, and some large, bushy, spiders and variants, and you're in business. And you will find that in periods of high wind, when the water surface is lashed and beaten with gusty blows, that solid old trout lose much of their caution and cavort on the surface like yearlings.

Several years ago, I put in a large part of one vacation on a stream that held only brook trout. I had no experience with these fish, and frankly had always thought of them as easy fish. After a week in which I caught only two trout, both under eight inches, I revised my thinking somewhat.

One day I was moping along the stream when I came upon a grizzled old angler sitting on the bank at one of the numerous bends. His pipe was going, his rod tip nodded drowsily, and the line disappeared into the water under the bank of the bend. Just drowning a worm, I thought.

Seeing me about to withdraw, the old angler motioned me over with his pipe. I went over to him, and gasped in surprise. In the grass beside him were a trio of colorful brook trout in the three-pound class.

Seeing my reaction, the old man grinned. "Not doing too well, son?"

"No," I confessed, "not doing a thing. Boy, those are nice, though."

"Sit down and I'll tell you about it," he said.

I sat down, and he told me about—or rather demonstrated—

his technique.

I had assumed he was fishing with bait. Instead, I found he was using an artificial nymph. He made a small ball of mud and imbedded his nymph in that. He would lower this gently into the water, and urge it, with the currents' help, back into the fish's lie. Then he would hold the line just taut while the water dissolved the mud around the nymph.

It was easy to imagine the rest. When the mud had dissolved, the action of the current on the taut line and leader would cause the nymph to move toward the surface in a completely lifelike manner. If there was a fish in the hold, he invariably was unable to resist this very natural presentation.

This is literally bait fishing with a fly. I've since used the method all over the country, for all kinds of trout, grayling, bluegill, and many others. It is especially effective for whitefish, with which I fill my smoker every year.

This method can be used at locations and under conditions where it would not be otherwise possible to use an artificial. It requires a modicum of skill in selecting the position, and in making the presentation. It definitely involves the selection of the proper fly; or nymph, if you will. And it invariably results in the taking of worthwhile fish in areas, and at times, where ordinary methods are useless. For these reasons, it cannot be overlooked by the advanced angler, even though it may not appeal to him.

The above brings to mind a dry-fly technique that I observed once, which, while it definitely works, and produces worthwhile trout, I cannot bring myself to like. I've used the method several times, always with good results, but always slink away from the stream after using this method, feeling I've somehow double crossed the fish and disgraced my brother anglers. Just why I should feel so, I don't know: the method is legal and sporting, but somehow, I don't feel right about it.

The fellow I first saw using this method was from Pennsylvania, and a dry fly angler only. He was fishing the Madison in the meadows and was doing all right by anybody's standards. From where I first spotted him, his technique looked odd, so I sat down and watched him through the binoculars for an hour or so. His style was definitely unusual.

He would make a prodigious cast, using the double haul. Then he would raise his rod, and strip in some line. After that he would fish the cast for some minutes, just jiggling the rod tip, but not otherwise moving. Also, his fly, to judge by his actions, did not drift with the current. It appeared to stay somewhere almost directly in front of where he was standing.

This unusual behavior impelled me to stash my binoculars away, and saunter nonchalantly down to where he was fishing. Fortunately, he proved friendly, as are most fly fishing nuts, and was happy to explain his system.

On the end of his tapered line was a six-inch loop of sewing thread to which was attached a small treble hook. About 12 or so feet up the line, a two-foot tippet of 2X nylon was fastened, directly to the line. A number 12 Ginger Quill was tied to this.

The angler cast this rig from across and slightly below the known or expected lie of the fish. The cast was long enough to allow the treble hook to reach the opposite bank upstream of the fish, and to catch in the grass. Then the angler held the rod upright and retrieved or gave slack to allow the fly to drift to the proper spot. At this point, enough tension was put on the line to cause the fly to skip and bounce on the surface. It required accurate adjustment to cause this to happen just upstream of the fish's lie. However, when this was accomplished, action was instantaneous and showy.

The instant the fish was hooked, the thread holding the treble hook broke, and the resulting fight was carried out in the regular manner.

This method is especially effective where the trout are lying near the opposite bank, or on the far side of conflicting currents. Nor does the bank have to be covered with grass—the treble will grab anything at all. You will lose a treble hook on every cast, but if you can abide the method, you will take worthwhile trout. Although perhaps not on every cast.

In concentrating on worthwhile trout, one of the first steps is to consciously avoid the holds, lies, and methods which attract small trout. Skip the shallow, slow riffles with gravel bottoms and no hiding places. Pass by the pools that have no cover for good fish. Be on the lookout for lies or holds that have sufficient depth, cover, and area to be attractive to larger fish.

Sometimes a stream will have few such lies. If so, it will contain few worthwhile fish. Such holds or lies that are suitable will often be widely scattered. Here, one does much walking and searching, but little fishing. There are two alternatives. One, construction of more good holding areas in the stream. Two, be content with smaller fish.

In concentrating on worthwhile fish, one must resign himself to the fact that much more of his time must be spent in fishing and less in casting. A lot more thinking will also be required. It is to avoid thinking that many anglers concentrate on casting rather than on fishing.

Also, to consistently take worthwhile fish, one may have to rid oneself of some prejudices. For instance some of the taking methods outlined in this book may not appeal to a good many anglers. If the angler refuses to use these methods, because of prejudice, or because they just do not appeal to him, no great loss will occur. There may be days when one of these despised methods is the only taking one, but these will be rare enough to occasion little pain. Besides, the angler should find some days that stump him, else he may grow blasé.

[5]

The Character of a Stream

The things about a trout stream that cause a man to frequent it, to select it over others if he has a choice, often have nothing at all to do with the size or numbers of the fish the stream holds. In fact, no fisherman that I know picks a stream to fish purely on the basis of where the best opportunity lies, although most fishermen do think that this is the reason for their selection.

One man is a timid wader; he will choose a stream with much back-cast room, or a feeble flow. Another revels in pitting his strength against the full flowing rush of a pounding current. He will be found thigh-deep in the fastest, heaviest runs his area affords. One likes solitude and quiet. He will seek out a small, overgrown brook, and probably spend more time observing nature than in filling the creel. Another is companionable; he likes the wide, big river with several other anglers always in view. And so it goes—there are endless variations in streams, and endless variations in the moods of anglers. Some anglers search for years before they find the stream that suits them, others find it their first year. Some never find it.

It took almost 20 years of searching, of fishing trout streams from Missouri to California, from New Mexico to Alaska, before I found a stream that satisfied my yearnings. By this time, I had begun to become interested in larger trout, and the fact that I found a stream that was at the same time esthetically pleasing, and held many large trout, was a bonus which I had not expected.

The source of a stream is always open to· question and debate. Is the source of a stream the headwaters of the longest tributary,

A winding, willow-lined stretch facing all corners of the globe.

or is it that tributary which supplies the largest volume of water to the whole? Is it that source which has the largest catch basin or watershed, or is it one which constantly supplies a regular amount to the stream? Who knows? Certainly not me. However, I have always felt that the source of a stream is that portion of a constantly flowing branch lying at a higher elevation than any other branch of that stream.

Based on that definition, the source of my long-sought trout stream lies far up on the nation's backbone, where the Continental Divide is almost a plateau. Lying just under the top of the eastern slope is a small, spring-fed lake. From it flows the headwaters of a noted and beloved trout stream. At this point it is quite small, an ice-cold trickle moping along through lodgepole pines so dense that the stream cannot be seen from above.

The watershed, although quite small, is at a very high elevation; and the snow, some six or more feet, lingers into late June. Thus, the flow of water is small, but steady.

Some mile or so before emerging from the dense woods, the stream tumbles down a series of benches, seeking the valley below —a valley which is itself a mile and a quarter above sea level. When it reaches the valley, the stream has become a mountain brook, running clear and swift, and incredibly cold, over a bed of golden stones. This character is maintained until it leaves the timbered head of the valley, and approaches the vast stretch of meadows that carry three-fourths of the stream's length.

It meanders through the valley with great leisure, its character vastly changed by the input from countless geysers, hot springs, warm ponds, mud pots, and the like. It takes no taint from this witches brew, either in color or purity. Instead, though it is considerably warmer than before it entered the meadows, it is also considerably more fishworthy. Three pounders lurk beneath its drifts and undercut banks, larger fish can be found around every bend of this winding stream.

After touring around Old Faithful, from which it receives several million gallons of warm water daily, the brook becomes a creek, and then, flirting with Daisy, Giant, Grotto, and Riverside Geysers, it passes under the bridge by Morning Glory Pool, and becomes a full fledged river.

In Biscuit Basin, it flows at ideal speed, facing every corner of the globe in turn. Big trout are here everywhere, under the drifts, beneath the banks, in the channels of the weed beds. Insect life is abundant and the fish rise more reliably here than anywhere I know.

The meadow grass grows tall, waist high in some areas. In the fall, after being touched by frost, it turns a deep golden brown that is pleasant to the eye and satisfying to the soul. The occasional patches of evergreen lend contrast.

Through Midway and Lower Basins it flows, becoming larger, but still retaining its dreamy character. Its temperature balance is maintained by the input of three cold-spring-fed creeks, and the hot overflow from the thermal pools and geysers, which on calm sunny days put up towering clouds of steam against a deep blue sky.

On cool cloudy days, and when the barometer is low, the mist hangs over the face of the water or just above the treetops, and the river assumes an evasive, secretive character. Though the river is nowhere more than a quarter of a mile from the road, one gets the feeling of being in a high, far corner of the world on these days.

At Nez Perce Creek, the river, which has been running out of sight of the road, makes a wide return swing and runs amiably beside the highway, broad, smooth, and well weeded, for several pleasant miles.

As it approaches the canyon, the stream begins to trot and then to gallop. It hobbyhorses down a series of rapids and chutes, then tumbles over the falls, as though in haste, or to make up for lost time. From the mouth of the canyon, it spills happily out into another wide and airy meadow, joins with another stream, and loses its identity forever.

The stream, of course, is the Firehole River in Yellowstone Park. At Madison Junction, below Firehole Canyon, it joins the Gibbon to form another notable trout stream, the famed Madison River.

The Firehole, with its many moods—its pitches, runs, glides and broads; its meandering course and its beauty of scenery—is many streams in one. This is true of almost all trout streams, but none that I know, in so short a space of miles, offers so much pleasant diversity as this one. And its ease of approach is another facet that I find charming, since the onset of the years and an old football knee, make me not so eager as I once was to go behind the mountain or over the ridge to find my chosen stream.

Although there are many trout streams similar in character,

A rocky breakover, well-oxygenated water, a fine hot-weather hold.

no two are exactly alike, and there are many types of character evidenced by trout streams. Within 50 miles of the Firehole are half a hundred trout streams, almost all showing a different face and personality.

The South Fork is a winding, willow-lined brook, crystal clear and excessively cold. It is a most difficult stream to fish when the fish are being uncooperative.

The mighty Yellowstone is huge for a trout stream, a hundred feet and more across in the Park, and three times that at Livingston. Its deep bends and long pools harbor hefty trout, but they are trout that require some catching.

The Grayling is a charming mountain brook, a stream for which one can develop a strong feeling of intimacy. It chatters down long riffles, tinkles in soft rills, and gurgles enticingly at the bends. Its midcanyon falls are singular in their wild beauty and solitude.

The various forks of the Snake are each as different from the other as is possible for streams to be. The main, or south, fork, is a lusty, brawling stream, long down from the really high places, arrogant in its power. It surges across the sagebrush flats of Jackson Hole, battering the bluffs in constant fury, then plunges relentlessly through the canyon on its way to meet its sister forks.

The Henry's Fork, by contrast, quashes and plods its way through marshes and bogs, looking more like a haven for waterfowl than a trout stream. It is milky but cool, and unapproachable in many areas. After it mingles with the river-sized flow welling up from Big Springs, it becomes a really fine, large mountain stream with mile after mile of riffles and runs stretching through evergreen-clad hills.

Duck Creek, just north of West Yellowstone, is a most unusual trout stream. Throughout its most productive sections, it glides with unbroken smoothness through twining willow and alder, over a mud bottom. It makes hardly a sound and only by a line of drifting bubbles is one aware of the current. It has many fine spawning riffles in the bitterbrush meadows far upstream, and it also resupplies itself from nearby Hebgen Lake. There are three- to five-pound browns to be had in its lurking pools and stealthy glides, but I find I cannot get interested in this strange stream, whose character is so different that it seems to have none.

When I get restless, and go across the mountains to Idaho, or across the plateau to beyond the Yellowstone, it is not the lure of larger trout that impels me. Rather it is the desire to fish a stream of different character than those to which I am accustomed.

Sometimes, I cross the Divide, loop down into Idaho, then back again up into the hills above the Centennial Valley—a country of serene and austere beauty. Here hundreds of nameless creeks flow down to Red Rock reservoir, and tiny, spring-fed ponds holding four pounders go unmolested by the seeking angler for years at a time.

A fine medium-deep glide, unusual for this mountain stream. Good dry-fly water.

Other times, I go up the canyon of the Gallatin and fish that mighty stream, which for some reason hosts mostly small trout, although many of them. But whatever stream I fish, I usually fish it because some facet of its character or personality is particularly pleasing to me that day.

I think this is true of most anglers. I have, many a day, fished with one companion or another who wanted to fish another stream, in a different area. Much of the time this was not because we were not catching fish, but because I or my companion, or both, felt out of tune with that particular stream. So, we traveled around, casting here, drifting there, until we found a stream that suited us, or until darkness fell. The latter was more often the case.

Why wander around, looking for a particular stream, when trout are to be had in the stream you are fishing? There are several reasons, not the least of which is that trout fishing in itself is a search for contentment. Then, one does better, or at least thinks so, on a stream that suits his mood.

Sometimes, weather may dictate a change of streams; a strong wind will cause one to seek out a more protected stream, or prolonged rain may pose a need to find a stream with a small watershed, or fast runoff. Low temperatures for an extended period may cause a drop of water temperature, and a reduction in fish activity. Then it is time to seek out a constant-level stream or one of warmer temperature. Quite often, though he has a legitimate reason and feels impelled to change streams, the angler may be unable to pinpoint his feelings. This brings on a hit or miss approach instead of a logically thought out one.

One time Ralph Richardson, Bill Phillips, and I went up on the Madison. It was early on a cold, drizzly September morning that presaged one of the most miserable winters in 50 years. The temperature was below freezing, and the rain was like icy needles.

We fished three miles of the Madison without raising a fish. If I hadn't had my thinking powers numbed by the cold, I might have figured the reason, but I didn't, and neither did Ralph or Bill.

"Let's go try the Grayling," Ralph suggested finally.

We drove back through town, stopping long enough to warm the inner man with a couple of Old Fashioneds, then went on up to the Grayling. Two hours there produced not a rise. Bill snagged his waders and Ralph lost his creel. The rain fell steadily, chilling our hands to the bone.

Ralph got restless again, and suggested a change in scenery, a drastic move this time. We piled into the car, looped back through West Yellowstone, crisscrossed the Idaho line and the Divide, and fished Culver Springs, Elk Creek, and Red Rock Creek. No dice. Ralph snagged his waders, and Bill lost a fly book. By this time, I was so numb I was no smarter than a stump and just about as active. When Ralph suggested Henry's Fork of the Snake, Bill and I just nodded.

We fished Henry's Fork 'til dark. We had been fishing twelve hours, in half a dozen fine streams, in a bone chilling drizzle, and we had had one strike. I forgot who it was that had it.

Bill and Ralph had been living in a tiny tent up at Madison Junction. I was staying in one of Roy Fitch's housekeeping cabins. The boys decided not to compound the felony, but to rent a cabin from Roy and get warmed up.

"I hope my wife has something good and hot for supper," I remarked, as Ralph tooled his Thunderbird back up the Divide, "like maybe some roaring hot chili."

We had been married long enough for my wife to have become a pretty good mind reader. When we arrived, the chili was ready, and roaring hot. The fire was crackling fiercely. After a couple of bowls of chili and an hour before the fire, we finally got thawed out.

"Dammit," said Ralph, "we've been even more stupid than usual. As cold as its been, and with that freezing rain and all, we should have been fishing the Firehole."

He was right. When we checked the reports next day, several good catches had been reported from the Firehole—none from any other stream in the area. The reason was basic. When I checked the temperature of the Madison the morning after our fiasco, something I should have done the day before, I found it a frigid 48 degrees. An hour later, the Firehole checked out just above 70. The temperature made all the difference; a trout doesn't get very enthusiastic at 48 degrees.

Sometimes the characteristic that one seeks in a stream is not found in the scenery, surroundings, temperature, or other facets of a stream's visible personality, but in the type of fish it holds. I for one will always go out of my way to fish waters that hold grayling.

The grayling is an easy fish, unable to withstand angling pressure. But, its predilection for the fly, its different type of strike and fight, and its flavor in the pan cause it to give a special character to waters it inhabits. It is soon caught out in streams, and one of the few times I fish in a lake is when I walk the five miles into Grebe Lake each year to fish for grayling. I am not especially fond of lakes, but Grebe is charming angling water, in delightful surroundings which give it almost the character of a stream.

When I think of the character of a stream, and its effect in influencing anglers to fish it, two streams in Alaska come to mind. These are both tributaries of the Tanana; they occupy adjoining watersheds, are almost identical in quality, and both are extremely

Superb dry-fly water, using both the classic approach (fishing the rise) or casting blind along the grassy banks with unorthodox dries. A large crane-fly imitation bounced upstream along the bank edge is a thriller.

fishworthy. The two streams are the Goodpaster and Clearwater rivers.

The Goodpaster is fairly typical of a northern stream of marsh-swamp origin, and so is the Clearwater. Both are almost identical in every respect. The Clearwater, as its name implies, is clear as gin. On the other hand, the Goodpaster is brown as ale, and this difference alone sets the two streams apart.

I should guess that over ten times as many anglers fish the Clearwater because it is clear. This is my reason, anyway, and I fished the Clearwater many times more than I fished the Goodpaster.

Not only was the clear stream more attractive to my eye, but I could observe what was going on, see the drift of the fly, and the reaction of the fish. This made the fishing much more entertaining and far more educational.

Not often are the differences in the character of streams so easily seen and readily evaluated. Mostly the differences are vague, the reasons why one is preferred over another elusive. But differences in character in streams are the main reasons for differences

A small willow-lined stream that harbors large trout. Very cold, very clear; both your art and artifice must be perfect to succeed here.

in angling pressure. Quite often a stream will get a reputation as an outstanding trout stream only because it is a delight to fish, and many anglers spend many hours working its waters. The overall catch is large, but the individual take is apt to be small. So, because of its character, and not because of its quality, a stream becomes famous.

Few persons will complain about this, however. As I've said, fishing is largely a search for contentment, and contentment is not dependent on the size of the catch.

Perhaps you may wonder why I, who profess to fish mostly for larger trout, write a chapter which appears to have nothing to do with that subject. The fact is, this chapter is a negative approach to teaching discernment. If you wish to bend your efforts toward taking worthwhile fish, and advancing as an angler, you must learn quickly the difference between the quality of a stream, and its more obvious aspect, which is character.

⟦6⟧

The Quality of a Stream

A trout stream, like a woman, is a jewel of many facets, It may be a thing of great beauty, but of no soul (and few trout) or it may be a blowsy slattern with no eye appeal and less fish appeal.

What the factors are that make one trout stream favored over another by man and fish are as many and varied as the reasons men give for the women they marry.

What is an ideal trout stream? If you want to start an uproar, the next time you are having a drink at the club, toss that question to the gentlemen. It will cause more debate by far than did "The Lady or The Tiger" and to about the same avail.

To be perfectly blunt about it, there is no such thing as an ideal trout stream, nor is there any angler who seriously thinks there is. Yet it is something we all love to talk about, to describe, to yearn and search for, and to keep saying we've found.

All good trout streams, east or west, mountain or meadow, have several things in common. One is relative purity of water (though purity can be carried to excess; some mountain streams and lakes are so "pure" that they are sterile, incapable of supporting even the lowest link in the chain of vegetation and creatures necessary to a trout's welfare).

Freedom from pollution is essential. So is an adequate dissolved oxygen supply. There are quite reliable tests for both of these factors, but are seldom made by fishermen. If the state stocks the stream with trout, it is relatively safe to assume that the stream is pure enough, and contains oxygen enough, to support a good head of fish.

Temperature is of some import, although I do not believe it is nearly so important as has been made out in the past. I have said that I think oxygen content is of more concern to a trout; it should also be stated that the warmer a given stretch of water, the less oxygen it is capable of holding. This does not always mean that a warm stream will contain less oxygen—in fact, it seems to be true only for those streams that have widely fluctuating temperatures. Streams varying considerably in level also vary in temperature; therefore, it should follow that a constant water level in a stream would imply a more nearly constant temperature. My experiments have indicated this to be correct for the most such streams. So, by implication, a stream that maintains a consistent water level regardless of temperature (high or low) should have a higher oxygen content than a similar stream that fluctuates in level and temperatures.

I have checked several spring-fed (constant level) streams against a like number of snow- and rain-fed (varying level) streams in the same general area for a period of several years. The constant-level streams exhibited a fairly constant temperature throughout the season; the varying-level streams also varied considerably in temperature.

I also ran oxygen-content tests on this series of streams. On days when the temperature of a given constant-level stream was the same as that of any of several of the varying level streams, the constant-level stream always had a higher oxygen content than any of the varying-level streams.

Some of the constant-level streams were fed by hot springs, some by cold. One stream exhibited a nearly constant 74 degrees throughout the season, another checked out at nearly 52 degrees all season. I expected that the colder stream would show a higher oxygen content, but the difference was minimal. Both streams were well supplied with fish, and generally, the fish seemed to average larger than any other streams in the group. Both were better supplied with the organisms and vegetation necessary for trout growth than were most other streams in the group, and both had abundant areas of fine holding water.

Holding water in quantity is a necessity if the stream is to be capable of withstanding today's angling pressure. Streams having few good holding areas are soon "fished out" even with heavy and repeated stockings. Lack of suitable holding areas cause trout to be vulnerable to all of those creatures which seek his capture—fish hawks, herons, kingfishers, mink, otter, predatory fish (including the larger members of his own kind), and of course man. Give a trout plenty of shelter and he will survive them all, and reproduce his kind. He may, if the food supply is short, remain small, but he will remain.

Food supply is the key to fish size. I have seen lakes in Alaska low in fish food supplies but containing unlimited numbers of trout. They were mature at fingerling size—one lake in particular did not contain a fish over four inches although there were millions of them. There are limits to the size a trout will grow to, even under ideal conditions. But bountiful food supply is a must if a trout is to attain anything like his proper size.

Too much food is possible; though not often found in streams, a few lakes provide so much natural food that fish taken on artificials are mostly the result of luck, even when the angler is of superior skill. This condition is so rare that it is almost never a problem.

For there to be a good food supply, the stream bed must be of gravel or larger stones, the soil fertile, the water pure and somewhat "hard" (having good mineral content). Limestone or "chalk" streams are good examples of "hard" water streams.

There must be some sort of haven for microorganisms—crevices in gravel, brush, sticks, weeds, reeds, something for the lowest link in the food chain to cling to and multiply. "Clean" bedded streams of sand, bedrock, or certain clay earths will not support these important microorganisms.

From the soil, weeds may grow to form havens for the micro-creatures—if that soil is of the right type. Logs, brush, waste wood of any kind may be placed in a "clean" bedded stream to improve it. But whether done by man or nature, there must be "holding areas" for the smallest creatures, or there will be no larger ones.

The microorganisms get their food from the water for the most part. Therefore, there must be food for them in the water. Certain vital minerals must be present; if they are not, the stream or lake will be barren. So, mineral content of a stream is a factor of first importance in stream quality.

Tests for "hardness" of water are easily made, and, with certain other observations added, can enable the angler or biologist to come up with a "pounds of fish per acre" figure that will give a good idea of the head of fish a stream can carry.

I first became interested in water "hardness" in 1952. I was fishing the Yellowstone River some 15 miles below the lake when a car stopped, and a man got out and began to make some tests at the stream edge. I had once worked in a boiler room and recognized that the tests were for water hardness.

The man introduced himself as Sid Gordon, stated he was writing a book on fishing, and inquired into my experiences in the Park streams.

I advised him that I had extensive experience only on four of them—the Gibbon, Firehole, Madison, and Yellowstone. Which of them, he inquired, did I think held the largest proportion of large fish, say fish over three pounds? I replied that in my opinion, the Firehole was superior in this respect. He said that this checked with his tests, and showed me notes to that effect.

We talked a good deal further on the subject, and Gordon kindly explained the use of his testing equipment. His book came out in 1955 and I immediately bought a copy. I recommend it as a must for the serious angler *(How to Fish From Top to Bottom,* by Sid W. Gordon, The Stackpole Company.)

Gordon's method for testing hardness is simple, easy to do, and is a reliable indicator of a stream's potential. I use it regularly as a check on the actual fishing, to see if a stream is living up to its potential. In most cases, I find it is not. When it is not, one of the other factors already mentioned is usually deficient.

When the stream contains occasional large trout, but only a fair number of legal size, I expect it to be deficient in holding water. If it contains large numbers of very small, barely legal fish, I expect it to lack havens for microorganisms. If it contains many (proportionately) sick or diseased fish, I suspect pollution. If it contains very few small fish, but has a fair number of large (three-pound up) fish, I suspect that the stream lacks suitable spawning sites.

Spawning areas are a must if the stream is to restock naturally. Thus, there must be a sufficient number of shallow gravelly riffles, or similar areas. Also, it is important that the stream not be too subject to freshet conditions just following the spawning period. This latter is one reason why a stream stocked with more than one species of trout will suddenly cease to produce its former

Water rich in minerals produces this type of weed cover. First-class trout water.

numbers of what was the dominant species, and show increased dominance of another species. This will be especially true if one species is a spring spawner and the other a fall spawner.

The same thing sometimes causes a formerly good fishing stream to go bad for a year or two. Unusual or unseasonal freshet conditions may have destroyed the major portion of a season's spawn; sometimes this happens two seasons in a row, and can almost destroy the fish crop.

These factors, then, control to a major degree the head of fish a stream can carry; purity, oxygen content, water level constancy, holding water, havens for microorganisms, hardness, and spawning areas. These are all qualities of a stream, their number, condition (good or poor) and relationship result in the overall quality of a stream. A change in any one of them will result in a proportionate change in the stream's overall quality.

I have used the term "head of fish" several times in this chapter. In its simplest terms, head of fish refers to the total weight of fish in any given area of a stream. It does not specifically mean size or numbers, but rather a combination of the two.

I believe that a stream which is constant, or nearly so, in the factors mentioned in this chapter will also maintain a fairly constant head of fish *in spite of angling pressure*. Remember that the term does not refer to size or to numbers, but to total weight.

A good case in point is that portion of the Madison River in Yellowstone Park.

In 1920, the average limit catch from this stream would check in at about four pounds per fish. In 1930 this average dropped to about three and one-half pounds per fish, in 1940 to three pounds, in 1950 to two and one-half pounds, and in 1960 to about one and one-half pounds per fish.

This steady reduction in the size of the average fish caught caused a cry that the famed Madison was being ruined, that it no longer was the stream it once was. Most of the outcry was raised by old timers who felt that the tremendous influx of new fishermen were harvesting fish that rightly belonged to them. This same outcry was heard in Walton's day on the famous English trout streams, and with just as much reason. That is, none.

On a stream that has proved itself over the years, as has the Madison, and which can be protected from pollution, as the Madison can, increased fishing pressure can reduce the size of the average fish caught, but overfishing cannot, of itself, ruin a stream. *Overstocking* can, by putting in more fish than the stream can adequately nourish, and if this policy is pursued for very long, the insect life will be destroyed, the food supply depleted, and in general, the stream will decline and cease to become fishworthy. It can only be restored by drastic overfishing, something most old-time trout fishermen say is going on all the time.

Overstocking a trout stream is no different than overstocking a cattle range. Take a ranch that will supply 1000 head of fine steers of 1000 pounds each for the yearly market. Make it produce 2000 head yearly without supplemental feeding. These steers will reach probably only 500 pounds or so. So, your ranch is still producing 1,000,000 pounds of meat yearly. However, it's not of quite such good quality as before.

Now, let's make it produce 10,000 head of steers yearly, without supplemental feed, and see what happens. We'll be selling our steers at about 300 pounds apiece if we let them mature, and we'll be ruining our range in the process by overgrazing. Erosion will follow, goodbye topsoil, with which goes any plant life. We will have sold two or five times the number of steers for the same total sum we got for the 1,000, and we will have ruined our ranch in the process.

The results of serious overstocking are long and lasting. Fortunately, this problem has long been recognized and is guarded against by conservation authorities.

To return to the decrease in the size of fish caught, this usually is the direct result of more anglers fishing the stream more hours, thus catching more fish. Therefore, fish are caught at an increasingly earlier age, and consequently are smaller. Or, to be perfectly fair, smaller than the average fish caught from the same stream ten or twenty years ago, but not smaller than a fish the same age caught in those years. Increasing the catch or take from a stream usually causes the fish to get larger more quickly, due to lack of competition for the available food supply. Scale readings and experiments by biologists have long confirmed this.

Lee Wulff has a theory that fish get smaller over the years not as a direct result of angling pressure, but rather because anglers keep the larger fish and return the smaller. This, he thinks, results in a breeding stock that is artificially restricted to smaller fish, which in turn causes the offspring to become a nation of runts.

I could agree if the breeding stock's small size was caused by disease, lack of food supply, or other natural causes. But in this case, the small size is due to relative immaturity, and I do not believe that, in fish, this will cause a significant decline in size over generations.

So, we have two conditions that can cause a reduction in the average size of fish caught, and neither of which is basically related to stream quality. One is overstocking; the other is overfishing. Of the two, overstocking can cause stream damage, and is more serious. A reduction in creel limits or a limiting of the number of anglers on specific streams will restore fishing quality on an overfished stream.

In the case of the Madison, especially that portion in Yellowstone Park, there seems very little likelihood that the number of anglers can be limited. Creel limits have been steadily reduced, but only after it became apparent that the size of the average fish caught had dropped considerably. This is a case of too little too late, especially since the limits in the state-owned waters continued to be high for a longer period.

The Madison is still a first-class trout stream, with numbers of good-sized fish present. There are probably nearly as many five pounders in its curving length as there ever were. Only, now, the catching of these is spread among almost 40 times the number of anglers as it was thirty or forty years ago.

The fate of the Madison parallels that of thousands of trout streams over the country. There seems to be no possibility of reversing the trend, since anglers are multiplying and stream lengths diminishing.

If this sounds pretty grim, and that I concur that the Madison is being ruined, perish the thought. This great stream is providing, and will continue to provide top-quality trout fishing. It is probable that the average catch will be composed of 1- to 1¼-pound fish, and the limit will be smaller; but this is still excellent fishing, considering the thousands of anglers whose recreation the stream supports. Also, I am of the opinion that when restrictions are lifted from Quake Lake, much of the pressure on the upper Madison will be eased.

In summing up, it can be seen that a stream's potential depends on its quality, but that the average size of fish caught is dependent mostly on angling pressure, angling skill excepted. In general, the more skillful or advanced angler will catch more of the larger fish present in any stream, regardless of stream quality.

There is more opportunity for man to improve fishing by improving stream quality than in all other areas together. There is literally no limit to the things that can be done to improve a stream, and, emphatically, I do not mean repeated stockings.

What I do mean is to improve those factors that have direct bearing on the health, growth, and reproduction of trout. In order to know where to start, one must first know what the present quality of the stream is, and then set out to improve those factors that are deficient.

If pollution exists, pollution abatement is naturally the first step. In some streams, this might be all that is necessary to make it fish-worthy. But if pollution has existed for a long time, it is possible that all beneficial vegetation and organisms have died, and then the problem becomes quite complicated.

Suppose a stream has been polluted for years, but legislation and/or education have eradicated the elements causing the pollution. The case here might be such that there is a stream bed and a water supply, and little else. Can such a stream ever become fish-worthy? Indeed it can.

First it would be necessary to survey the stream to see what qualities remained, and in what condition they were in. Oxygen supply, mineral content, and adequacy of year-around flow would be the first things to check. If the stream fluctuated greatly in levels, the watershed might have to be rebuilt. There are several ways to do this, none easy.

One, beaver can be imported into the headreaches. Protected from man and other predators, they will flood the upper areas, increase the height of the water table, and promote ground cover growth. Freshet conditions will be to some extent controlled. Vegetation will soon flourish.

The above is probably the cheapest way to begin to restore a watershed. To this should be added seeding of the area by airplane (grass, trees, and shrub seeds) and perhaps sodding of some badly eroded areas.

It will take longer, but eventually the beaver will accomplish the complete rebuilding of the watershed. How long? It depends on the conditions. From 10 to 25 years, perhaps. Time means nothing to a beaver.

Eventually, the upper watershed will be restored, and then, the beaver must be controlled, or he will block all spawning areas. As long as some are left, and the spread of the beaver controlled, trout will continue to reproduce and flourish.

Downstream, we still have a stream bed, and now, a more reliable water supply. Suppose the oxygen content is low. Water literally beats oxygen into itself, so some man-made rapids, or series of low falls are in order. These, constructed in the shallower, swifter stretches, also deepen the water and act as holding areas.

Mineral content? Lime in great and small chunks is the best answer. Any source of lime is good. Sea shells (clams or oysters) will help. Regular commercial fertilizers will work, but are prohibitively expensive. An increase in the amount of fertilizer used on crops on the watershed will help, as will pasturing of additional animals along the stream. Your state biologist can tell you what minerals need to be added to make the stream more fishworthy. Also, in many cases, the state will help pay all, or a large part, of the cost to supply minerals for such use.

Aquatic vegetation? In low-water, slow-moving streams, be careful with this one. It will provide havens for microorganisms, and will add oxygen; but weeds may spread to such an extent that they choke the stream, or raise the temperature to a critical point by slowing the flow. Again, your state biologist is the man to consult.

Adding insects, after the mineral content is high enough, is usually a case of seining such insects from other, better-stocked streams, and transporting them to the stream being improved. This should be done at least three years before restocking—and after any poisoning campaign to remove rough fish. Insects taken at different times from different streams offer the better possibility of getting a good stock established.

Holding water improvements offers vast opportunities. Again, in streams of low flow and slow current, care must be used so as not to further slow up the current, although this is not dangerous, if the stream has an adequate dissolved oxygen supply. Rocks and logs can be placed in a stream in such a manner as to increase, or slow the current flow, deepen or shallow the water, and still provide good holding areas. If a stream is to undergo heavy angling pressure, some completely unfishable areas of holding water should be built to protect a brood stock. Ideally, such areas should be located near good feeding water.

In building holding areas, if limestone is available, and the stream is deficient in that mineral, chunks of limestone should be used to build holding areas, thus deriving a triple benefit. In addition to holding areas for trout, shell type insects will seek out such stones, and they, in turn will provide trout food.

Spawning areas usually take care of themselves, once the main body of a sick stream has mended itself. But if the small tributaries are silted because of erosion, "forcing cones" can be built to cause current flow strong enough to scour the gravel clean. These log or rock devices are simply and cheaply built, and provide other benefits as well.

The above steps are some that can be taken by the angler to improve his sport. They are quite general in nature, because each stream, sometimes each separate stretch of a stream, may pose a different problem, and the exact nature, and therefore the treatment, can be determined locally.

Sportsmans associations, Rod and Gun Clubs, and conservation organizations, are some of the units that can be called on for help. In some cases, as has been done, a local organization could be formed for the sole purpose of saving and revitalizing a trout stream. Certainly, it is going to be up to the angler, more and more, to be increasingly responsible for the quality of his sport, and this is directly dependent upon the quality of the streams he fishes.

[7]

Dry Flies and Methods

I think it is probably clear by this time that I am not especially fond of dry fly fishing as a way to take good trout. I do not mean to imply that it cannot be done; I have done it, but, nearly all the good trout I've taken by conventional dry fly methods have been the result of happy accidents.

For several years I fished the dry fly almost exclusively. I enjoyed nothing more than seeing the deliberate rise and confident take of a completely fooled trout. I took my share of fish and perhaps more, and I was having fun. But after a few years it was unwillingly forced upon me that I was catching mostly 12- and 14-inch fish in streams that abounded with three- or four-pounders.

It is true that I haven't the slightest interest in angling for record breakers. It is equally true that I am not interested in angling for twelve-inch trout in streams containing an abundance of much larger fish.

I used the term "conventional dry fly methods" at the beginning of this chapter. By this, I mean, actually, the use of the closely imitative fly and the dragless float, the method still used by the majority of dry fly anglers.

Without abandoning dry fly fishing, I have changed my methods. No more the delicate, winged, jauntily cocked mayfly types, no more endless false casting—the ritual of drying, oiling, and "blowing" up the fly before it can be fished.

My first move away from conventional methods was a rather wide swing. I commenced to tie and use floating deer·hair mice and large beetle types. Regular dry fly fishermen looked at me in horror, and edged away from me as though I had the plague, when I happened to mention my choice of lure. Shunned or not, it made little difference to me. I was not catching nearly so many trout as formerly, but those I did catch were no twelve-inch yearlings.

After a year or so, I modified my tactics and lures, then gradually began to add other types of lures until arriving at my present method of "dry fly" fishing.

I seldom fish to other than an individual rise, and not then until I have made fairly certain it is a worthwhile fish. Keep in mind that this term, as used herein, refers to fish of a pound or more.

I do not wish to leave the impression that angling is a business— a cold blooded affair of selecting a certain fish, then calmly attempting its capture. I angle for fun, for sport, for diversion, escape—or something of all of those. I can be very happy just to be fishing in those wonderful surroundings that are invariably found around trout streams.

But, just as keeping score is important to add zest to golf, so is the catching of sizeable fish important, to me at least, in adding zest to angling.

To a great extent, in dry fly fishing I angle for specific fish, almost never for just any fish. However, I don't make a career of one fish. Should my ordinary blandishments fail, I move on, knowing full well there will be other fish and other days, for here lies one of the major joys of angling, the anticipation of tomorrow or the "next time."

The first fly added to my mice and beetle collection was an all deer hair pattern, tied in the general shape of the Grey Hackle, but with tail, body, and hackle all of brownish-grey deer body hair. I called it Shaving Brush. It resembles that earlier and better known pattern, the Goofus Bug.

This fly was developed to give me a generally fly-like lure for the heavy runs and fast-water stretches. It works well in these places, but will also take fish in glassy smooth water, although it was not meant to be used here.

Later on, a grasshopper pattern was added, and last but not least a deer hair—bucktail pattern, the Montana Stone Fly. This last one has produced more big fish than any dry fly I've ever used.

The fly was designed specifically for use in that stretch of the

Madison from Hebgen Dam downstream to the mouth of the canyon, the stretch now covered by Quake Lake.

This was big, rough, brawling water; it had tremendous stone fly hatches in the spring. It also had occasional small hatches later on, with a fly now and then seen as late as August. Whenever there was even a single adult of this fly on the water, my big bucktail-looking dry fly would produce.

I have since caught whopping good trout on it in clear-water ponds and lakes. Some of these places have no stone fly hatches, so what the fish take it for I don't know. But I've no doubt they take it for a real fly; a good many fish caught on this pattern have swallowed it and have been hooked deep in the throat.

I believe action is the reason the fish take this fly to be something alive. Floating semi-submerged in rough water, the long bucktail wing moves with the water, giving the appearance of swimming. On still waters, each slight air current flutters the winghair, imparting life to the fly.

The first sizeable fish I caught on this fly was on the Madison just before it leaves the Park. Joe Johnson and I went down for the late evening fishing. We had an hour of sport on the wet fly, then about a half hour before dark, things went dead.

I continued to use the wet fly, but Joe, always restless, changed over to the dry fly. After trying a couple of patterns, he put on a Muddler Minnow, simply because it was getting dark and he wanted a fly he could see. At once he took a nice fish, and called across the stream to me to put on a Muddler.

I had no Muddler, but did have two of these big stone flies, one a number four, 3X long, and a number 2, also 3X long. I put on the number four, and dropped it just below a big rock out in the main current.

The fly floated down, then started to drag across, skipping on the broken water. On the third skip a 2½-pound rainbow smashed it. It took several minutes to land this fish; by then it was nearly dark.

Two or three casts produced nothing; then, a fish hit hard just as the fly touched the water. I struck too hastily, the fly sailed back and struck the top of an exposed rock, breaking the hook at the barb.

Quickly, I tied on the number 2, and in my haste apparently did a poor job on the knot. On the fourth or fifth cast, the fly suddenly disappeared and I was fast to a heavy fish. But only for seconds; he turned on a strong downstream run and I felt the line go slack. Almost instantly, a fish jumped in midstream below me, a big shouldered brown of some five pounds, the big fly hanging from the corner of his jaw. He turned upstream and jumped twice more. Joe, now able to see the fly, which was on his side, thought I still had the fish on, and quickly reeled in so I would have a clear field. I believe he was more disappointed than I at the loss of the fish, for it was long after dark before I could persuade him to leave the stream.

In dry fly fishing, I will be among the first to admit that I believe pattern is of great importance, far more so than in wet fly fishing. But it is not all-important. Just as in wet fly fishing, I think size and natural presentation are of distinct importance. Patterns and natural presentation have been with us for years; it is in size of fly that I differ from most dry fly anglers.

This is a natural consequence of angling strictly for sizeable fish. Larger trout do not feed indiscriminately, nor do they feed regularly on the surface as do the yearlings. However, these big fellows will come to the surface for food—if the food is large enough to be worthwhile, and real acting enough to leave them unsuspicious.

Our long-held beliefs that trout are dainty feeders is part of our English heritage. In that country, the supply of large aquatic insects ranges from scarce to nonexistent. Therefore, English trout feed on small surface flies and English writers write about taking trout on such small stuff.

We followed along blithely for many years before such men as Koller, Jack Knight, and Al McClane began to indicate in their writings that England is not necessarily America.

In the West, the trend away from English dry fly tradition started sooner and veered wider than it did in Eastern America; but fewer Western writers appeared, so the word was sometime getting out.

The Trude flies, developed around 1903, were among these first steps away from the English influence. In spite of their effectiveness, relatively few fishermen used them. The dry fly fisherman is a hide-bound sort, usually a lover of tradition. He changes unwillingly, if at all.

Dan Bailey of Livingston, Montana, has been instrumental in

A deep, quiet "hole." Fine dry-fly water, with water depth and undercut banks providing cover.

influencing the thoughts of many Western anglers. He developed offshoots of the Trude and Wulff flies, and spread the word that they would take big trout. Some few followed his advice, but in general, the Western dry fly man stuck to his English methods and matching the hatch.

The Wulff and Trude fly derivations led to more flies having hair, especially deer hair, in their makeup. Among the more successful of these were the Bi-fly, Goofus Bug, Sofa Pillow, and those big, bass bug appearing flies, the Rough Water series. A Western grasshopper became popular.

About the time I began to be awakened to the possibilities of big, rough-appearing dry flies, I was shown a catch of whopping trout by Glenn Goff of West Yellowstone.

These trout had been taken on the South Fork, a stream of which a fine angler once wrote, "both your art and your artifice must be perfect if you are to succeed here." Yet these trout, 12 of them, averaging four pounds apiece and not one less than three, had been taken out of the crystal-clear waters of the South Fork on size 6 Goofus Bugs and Western Grasshoppers by Glenn and his guests.

Lightning didn't strike at once, though. Things percolated around for about three or four years before I finally "went big fly." Once I did, and compared the fish I was catching with those I had been catching, there was no turning back.

I do not advocate the use of large flies on streams where no large naturals, aquatic or terrestrial, are ever taken by trout. Nor do I say that very small flies will not take a large trout. The writings of Bergman, LaBranche, and fellows like Vincent Marinaro are amply filled with instances of large trout being taken on small flies. Except for certain instances on specific streams, I remain convinced that such happenings are the result of happy accidents.

As far as matching the hatch, I haven't seen a dozen real, honest-to-goodness hatches in over 30 years of trout fishing. Even during those times, I have found that it was difficult to take the really good fish. There are several reasons for this. Sometimes the hatch could not be matched. Sometimes the trout were actually taking a different fly than the noticeable hatch, and this was discovered too late. Other times, the very number of flies on the water made it improbable that the artificial would be selected by the fish.

Actually, the best dry fly fishing I experienced in earlier years came on those days when only a few scattered flies were hatching. This made it easy to mark down individual rises, and fish only those rises which appeared to be made by good fish.

Thus, although my method has changed but slightly, my choice of fly has changed greatly. I still seek out individual rises of worthwhile fish, but I present him with a much different bill of fare.

I have had good success with my big flies on days when the fishing appeared absolutely dead. On these days, after trying the wet fly and nymph in all their variations, and after searching the surface for dry fly activity and finding none, the day has been saved by heavy-handed fishing with the large dries.

It is an unusual business, this method, almost completely at variance with standard dry fly practice. The fly is slapped down hard on the water. Drag is deliberately courted, or accentuated. The fly may be jerked and twitched on the surface. Skittering and bump casting are both used. Sometimes one of these actions will raise a trout, sometimes another will. Occasionally, all of them work, and invariably, the trout are good ones.

One more or less conventional fly which has given good results is the large spider type. By large, I mean a number 6 or 8 hook and a hackle spread of two inches. I also prefer them a bit more heavily hackled than usual.

I first saw this type of fly in Bob Carmichael's shop in Jackson Hole in 1948. Roy Donnelly was responsible for their use, as he had developed the pattern a couple of years earlier. Those big Donnelly Variants and spiders did great execution on the turbulent waters of the Snake, but after I left there, I used them little, except on some of the heavier flowing streams in Alaska. The light still hadn't dawned.

The light did dawn about ten years later. I had been using larger dries for a season or two and was gradually becoming aware of their excellence in taking larger fish. But tradition and early teaching still had too strong a hold.

The hold was broken one day on the Firehole, after I had spent six hours looking for rises and seeing none. I had sat down on the bank of a long, canal-like stretch, my wadered feet in the water. Across the stream, up against the far bank, a fish suddenly rose; another rose instantly just above it, and a third, a brown of two pounds or so, came clear of the water just upstream of the first two. Then the same sort of activity commenced on my side, near where I was sitting. A little observation revealed the cause of the commotion.

A light hatch of huge crane flies was responsible. These flies were large enough to span the palm of ones' hand, and were of a fiery red-orange color. They were fluttering upstream near the banks, just off the water, and the trout were jumping for them like crazy.

I had some Brown Spiders in my box, but they were regular spiders on 14 and 16 hooks, with about size 8 hackle. I took several fish on them, but they just weren't big enough, and I began to wish I had some of Roy Donnelly's big variants.

Later on I made up some, in fiery red-brown. At certain times these huge flies produce the kind of fishing that can give a man heart failure. Bouncing them along close to the bank, I've had a half dozen rises in as many seconds, with some of the fish coming clear of the water in their eagerness to seize the fly. And not just any fish, but browns up to 3½-pounds. On two occasions, I've hooked trout of this size while the fly was in the air. This creates the same feeling that I get when a covey of quail explodes unexpectedly under my feet.

We have in the West several fly tiers of merit, who are not unknown nationally. I've already mentioned that two of them, Donnelly and Bailey, introduced large flies some years ago.

In checking, I found that nearly all of our better Western tiers have introduced and used large dries of somewhat unusual appearance. I do not propose to make a complete list, but some mention should be given to men like the late Don Martinez who pioneered variations of the Trude flies, and the Rough Water series, and Wayne Buzek and his Deschutes Stone Fly; these men and others have been for years catching large trout on walloping big dry flies, and have been trying to promote their use.

Western trout-stream insects are often very large. This Pteronarcys californica *nymph—and its imitation—are nearly two inches long.*

Large dry flies are needed to match this Pteronarcys californica *adult. This giant stonefly, locally called a "salmon fly," is nearly two inches long.*

Along the Gunnison, in Colorado, anglers have long been using a huge dry fly called "willow fly." Actually, there are two different species imitated by these "willow flies" in Colorado. One imitation is concerned with the Chauliodes species of the fish fly; the other is an imitation of the Pteronarcys species of stone fly. Both are top takers of large fish.

Along the Feather River, in California, they call their dry imitations of the giant stone fly "salmon flies"—a misnomer used throughout the West, particularly Montana and Idaho. In some areas the adult dobson fly is called "salmon fly" and in others, both the stone and dobson fly are called salmon flies. In most of these areas, the use of the dry imitation is restricted to spring—mid May and early June—so ingrained is the idea of "matching the hatch."

Some dry fly anglers I have met appear reluctant to admit that they use grasshopper imitations. No angler of my acquaintance will admit to using imitations of crickets or beetles. Yet these three flies—or lures, if you prefer—are the only ones I know that will consistently raise good trout when no rise or hatch is on.

Once, as an experiment, I fished two days on the Madison, exclusively on the surface, but never once using a conventional dry fly. I used deerhair mice, crickets, beetles, grasshoppers, cork and deerhair bass bugs, and floating cork and quill minnows.

I did not catch many fish. But three quarters of those I did catch were at least twenty inches in length; none was less than fourteen.

I fished all sorts of water—glassy, canal-like meadow stretches, glides, riffles, bouncing runs, and deep pools. Only the pools failed to produce. Every type of lure took at least one fish.

It may be that these "dry fly" methods seem crude. Along that line, the Letort anglers who fish that fine limestone water with imitations so small that a size 16 looks like a sailboat always await the grasshopper season eagerly, and have for years depended on grasshopper imitations for late summer sport. They do not seem to find it strange to switch from size 22 to size 8 or 10 when that is what is called for. Nor has anyone ever called their methods crude. Their only criteria is that their floating flies represent a natural and that it take fish.

That sums up the code of dry fly fishing for larger trout.

[8]

Mountain Stream, Meadow Stream

In fishing, as in nearly everything else, seldom is anything all black or all white. Thus, it is somewhat dangerous to label a stream as mountain or meadow, since most trout streams will exhibit a combination of the characteristics of both types.

Most trout fishermen, I believe, when they think of meadow streams, think of the chalk streams of England or some of the more canal-like streams of France. Conversely, when they think of mountain streams, it is the more precipitous ones of Colorado or the Adirondacks that come to mind.

While we have some streams in this country that do resemble the chalk streams of England, they are located, in most cases, in mountainous areas. Because of our latitude, our trout streams are located at higher altitudes than those of England.

So, it can be seen that a stream cannot be identified as a mountain or meadow strictly on its location. How can it be so identified, and what is the purpose of such classification?

The purpose is twofold. First, mountain and meadow streams, even in the same general area, are apt to have somewhat different forms of insect life, and the prevailing form in one type stream will not be the same as that in the other. Secondly, partly because of the insect differences, and for several other reasons, a different style of fishing must be used.

As far as classifying a stream as mountain or meadow, it depends mainly on the appearance; but one also must consider the factors above. A stream is not a meadow stream just because it flows through some pastoral looking valley for most of its length.

A gliding run on a small meadow stream. Boulders, which cause ripples, provide cover for large trout.

Nor is it a mountain stream just because it lies at an elevation of several thousand feet.

A mountain stream is one that has a considerable amount of rapids, or shallow, swift, rock-filled stretches which are unfishable and unfishworthy. Its fish holding areas are apt to be scattered, with unfishable stretches between. Its current will be swifter, it will tend to be shallower and its banks narrower than a meadow stream. Such a stream will be more exhausting to fish because it requires more walking, and usually over rougher terrain.

In the Sierra of California, the Rockies of Colorado, the Selway and Bitterroot of Idaho and Montana, these swift-running, narrow, boulder-strewn streams are numerous. They are more easily fished with the salmon egg or the worm than with the fly. Occasional deep pools may hold large trout, but in general, though sometimes numerous, the trout run disappointingly small.

In fishing these streams with a wet fly, at least three, perhaps four, techniques are necessary. In general, the fly is less successful here than bait or hardware, and is not as effective as is the fly in the meadow stream.

I have fished this type of stream many a happy––and many an exasperating––hour. So demanding are they of the proper technique that it is usually feast or famine. Either you catch nothing or you get your limit.

The technique most generally successful for me is one of which I am not particularly fond. A streamer or bucktail is used. Fishing the quieter, deeper stretches, the fly is cast out, allowed to sink and lie on the bottom a minute or so. Then it is retrieved in six- or eight-inch pulls, with occasional pauses. A fly that resembles the prevalent minnow, or small trout, is usually the best choice.

When this method produces results, but not as good fishing as could be expected, a change of fly is in order. A much larger or much smaller fly may work. Sometimes a switch to a somewhat outlandish pattern will pep things up.

Several years back, I designed an all bear-hair pattern for silver salmon in Alaska. It was meant to be an imitation of the eulachon (hooligan, candlefish), and when first made it was a credible imitation. But it was in four colors, and bear hair is notoriously difficult to dye so that it will not fade or change color.

In time the action of sun and water changed two of the colors to produce a rather sickening looking affair resembling no fish I know of. Yet, when the fish are being choosy about streamer patterns, this oversized monstrosity sometimes produces surprising results.

A large marabou pattern is good under the aforementioned conditions. An all-brown wing with gold body and large jungle cockeye works best for me. All black is next, with yellow and white not too effective.

Small things often spell the difference between success and failure. Sometimes, all that is necessary to start the fish hitting, with this sunken streamer, is to let it lie on the bottom longer. On some occasions, a wait of five minutes before starting the retrieve has worked when a wait of two or three minutes failed. Also, sometimes the length or speed of the jerks of the retrieve is all-important.

At times, the hand-twist retrieve, slowly and rather steadily, is the answer. However, when this is the case, a nymph-type fly usually works better than the streamer-bucktail.

This brings us to the second form of presentation, the rising-to-the-surface method. In this one, some form of nymph or large, sparse wet fly is the choice. This, like the streamer, is cast well out,

A gliding run and feeding riffle. Trout will be in one or the other, but seldom in both.

but where the streamer is usually cast across, or quartering down-stream, the nymph is cast up, or quartering upstream.

Again, the fly is allowed to lie on the bottom for a while, if it will do so. If the current speed is such that it drifts the fly, and will not allow it to settle, it should be retrieved just a trifle faster than the current. Both a steady retrieve and slight twitches should be employed until the taking method is found.

If the fly will come to rest on the bottom, leave it there at least a minute. Then retrieve with lifts and dips of the rod tip, "walk-ing" the fly along the bottom. These lifts and dips should be quite deliberate. A long, fine leader is an asset here.

The above two methods are just about limited to the slower moving, deeper sections of mountain streams. The only consistently effective method I know of for the faster stretches is the weighted-fly, persistent-cast method.

In the days before Quake Lake gobbled up that section of the Madison in the canyon, this was the most successful method, day in, day out, on this stretch, which was fairly typical of mountain streams.

Much of the water was fast enough to be unfishable with the fly. Other stretches would have pockets of fish-holding water in much larger unfishable stretches. The fish in these pocket holds were large, shockingly so, to one used to such streams in other areas. They would average four pounds, I should think, and seldom were smaller than two and one-half. Usually, there was just the one fish in each pocket.

The current on all sides was a veritable maelstrom. There was no possibility of "reading" the water so as to know where to cast to obtain proper drift of the fly. It was strictly trial and error, or as the dry fly man would say, "chuck it and chance it."

After a dozen or so casts, you could begin to get an inkling of the effect of the water on the line and leader, and adjust your position so as to allow a decent drift of the fly. Sometimes, of course, several moves might have to be made before the right position was found.

A large fly was a must. Firstly, the dominant insect was the giant stone fly, *Pteronarcys californica*. Secondly, the fly lingered only briefly in the area of the hold. Therefore, a fly that could be easily seen was necessary.

The number four black wooly worm was good, but most any

A deep run above a breakover—several types of water in a short stretch. Each must be fished differently.

large dark fly with grizzly or grouse hackle would serve in these particular areas. In the infrequent large pools, the choice of fly was a completely different story.

Very little manipulation of the fly is possible under these conditions. About all that can be done is to hope that one drift out of a dozen will pass through the hold in a natural manner, and that the fish might not have his attention elsewhere at the time. Repeated drifting of the fly through the same area is necessary; sometimes half a hundred drifts are needed before the strike will come.

The fourth method for fishing mountain streams is one seldom seen. It was shown me by Larry Phillips of El Portal, California. Larry is among the best mountain stream fishermen of my acquaintance. The area that he fished, and which I consider to be most typical of all the mountain streams I know, was that section of the Merced River from the Arch Rock Ranger Station to the confluence of the South Fork.

Larry had no name for his method, but I call it the continuous drift. The fly is cast across and down; then the angler follows along, endeavoring to keep the fly moving at the exact speed of the current. It isn't easy.

No attempt is made to control the direction of the fly, it is allowed to drift, willy nilly, wherever the capricious current takes it. The entire effort is expended in trying to achieve a sort of water-borne weightlessness. If this is achieved, the fly drifts and looks completely natural. Many good lies will be missed by the fly, but for the ever-moving school of fishermen, of which there are plenty, this is an effective method of presentation. Since the angler is at all times upstream of his quarry, a long line and leader are necessary, as well as quiet and skillful wading. It isn't necessary to cast more than once every ten minutes or so.

Another angler who fished this stretch used a completely different technique to achieve results as good as Larry's. I call this method "pot shooting," for the angler flicked a series of short casts into all the likely areas, picking the fly up after a short drift and shooting it into another spot. It requires exceptional casting ability, for the angler is working swiftly with a very short line. Neither the pickup nor the delivery can be bungled.

What about the dry fly on mountain streams? I think it probably the poorest of all for attracting good fish. Also, here again, exceptional casting skill is called for, to deliver the fly lightly, smoothly, and exactly, so that it will float the smooth and eschew the rough. Frankly, it is my opinion that of the many men who fish this method most do so because they enjoy the precision necessary for the cast and drift, and regard the catching of trout as a nice but not necessary adjunct—something like tournament casters and target shooters.

If you must fish the dry fly in mountain streams, you can derive a lot of enjoyment from it; but unless you are an exceptionally advanced angler, you will take few worthwhile fish. I have seen a few such anglers in my day. I am not one of them, but recognize them when I see them.

One man I met once when I was in the ranger service was the most accomplished dry fly fisherman I have ever seen. He also is the only one I know who habitually took limits of 14- to 18-inch trout from mountain streams. He did it in the classic manner— the stealthy approach, the short perfect cast with only the fly on the water, and a short, dragless float.

In addition to his approach and casting ability, he could read water with the best, and he placed nearly all his faith in delivering one perfect cast to each hold. If that cast failed to produce, he

Deeply undercut banks make excellent holds for large trout on this fine meadow stream.

*A superb stretch of meadow stream. Good current speed allows both wet-
and dry-fly fishing, as needed.*

moved on—to return and try that spot another day. Oddly enough,
in meadow streams, where his classic dry fly methods should have
been supreme, he failed more often than not, simply because there
was nothing like a normal hatch at any time, in the meadow streams
he fished. His methods were not suitable to imitating terrestrials,
nor were his flies.

Meadow streams, or meadow stretches of mountain streams,
are habitual producers of large trout. While the rainbow does not
favor them so much, the brown will choose a meadow stream if
he has a choice, and will wax fat and live long. He will feed most
of his life on insects, provided there is an adequate supply of such
food in his area. Otherwise he will eat minnows, mice, and other
trout smaller than himself. However, most meadow streams have
reasonably good insect stocks.

The larger fish tend to seek the deeper waters, the quieter pools.
They prefer a secretive and hidden lie, and in many meadow streams
this is apt to be beneath undercut banks or limestone ledges.

The Madison flows for most of its fishable length through
meadows of one sort or another, although some of them, Missouri
Flats for instance, bear no resemblance to the traditional cow
pasture that most people call meadows.

A gliding run pouring over a jam of logs and rocks. Excellent holding water on a small mountain stream.

The proximity of roadways causes this area to be subject to heavy fishing pressure. Because of the glassy surface, the average angler does not do well here.

Where the Firehole and Gibbon join to form the Madison, the Madison is a meadow stream by just about any definition. The old canyon stretch, of some ten miles, was big, brawling, typically mountain stream. With the disappearance of this section, the West lost one of the truly great stretches of mountain stream. Quake Lake may produce more and bigger fish, but it's just a lake, not what has been called by many one of the greatest stretches of trout water in the world.

So, what remains of the Madison is essentially meadow stream, and it includes nearly all of a meadow stream's characteristics. In some places it will alternate glides, riffles, pools, and runs. In others it flows with the deceptive smoothness of a canal. Do not be misled; there is current there, one that's cantankerous beyond belief. Against the elbows of its frequent bends, you will find deep swirls, always spots for good fish. Occasionally, it breaks into a gallop, but it is a restrained gallop. It features mile after mile of almost continuously fishable water and thousands of good lies.

In a stream such as this, all an angler's skill is called for; it is you versus the open river, and trout that have grown wise through experience.

A diversity of approaches and techniques are needed to cope with the river's changing moods. In the meadows near Madison Junction, the classic dry fly approach works well much of the time. Terrestrials of all kinds and deer hair mice, gently delivered and drifted near the grassy banks, do great execution at times.

Further down, but still in these Alpine-like meadows, there are great deep holes, where the deeply sunken nymph and the rising-to-the-surface methods does well. Here too, at times, a slowly twitched streamer will work. It is the only section of this stream where I would use this method with any confidence.

In the area from a mile above the cable car crossing, to where the stream emerges from the Park at Baker's Hole is a different type of water. Not so deep as the meadow pools, and a little faster than the broads, it is ideal wet fly water. The bottom is composed of large stones, with now and then a series of large boulders. However, the banks are grassy and undercut in typical meadow-stream fashion and many are the fine trout that rest in these lies, watching the passing current for food.

The natural drift with the deeply sunken fly works best in this type of water. The current is strong, though not swift, and a long leader and weighted fly improve your chances. In the shallower sections, there are some depressions, which are hidden from the eye of the average angler but which contain good fish. The natural drift is again the best bet, but other methods will work. Also, for some reason unknown to me, the fish in these lies will come up almost to the surface for the fly.

Below Quake Lake, across Missouri Flats, to Ennis and beyond, are some 60 miles of riffles, runs, and pools—one after the other. Typical mountain stream tactics work well here, although the deeply sunken, naturally drifting fly produces the best fish. But dry fly, streamer, and nymph, will all produce at given times, and all are used with success.

Of late, more terrestrials are being used in this section. This is in line with conditions; the sage-covered flats and grassy valleys produce a host of land borne insects. Grasshoppers are present in droves, and a grasshopper imitation is always a good bet in summer on a meadow stream.

Dan Bailey developed a couple of his Wulff variations for this section, and the Sofa Pillow was born here. A big, bushy dry fly to imitate the giant stone fly is a killer, as is the Muddler Minnow. I've been speaking here of the Madison, but what I say is applicable to similar streams throughout the West.

The Bi-Fly, used as a wet, is one of the better producing wet flies; the wooly worm in dark olive, and in black are hard to beat. You need use nothing smaller than a size 6 if you are after the worthwhile fish. The Montana and Bitch Creek nymphs are also takers of good fish. I've had little success with the streamer, and this goes for nearly all such streams.

In his book, *Trout*, Ray Bergman mentions a style of fishing on the Owens River of California which is locally known as "Floating the Bank." This is Larry Phillips's continuous drift adapted to meadow streams. A much shorter line is used, and the fly is kept very close to the bank, with the angler staying well back. Rod and arm are extended, and a stealthy tread is a must. A large nymph-type fly will normally be a good choice. This type of presentation is good anywhere where there are undercut banks. It can be used with the dry fly, especially terrestrials. It is very killing early in the morning during hot weather to use an imitation grasshopper.

A slight variation on the above method is good for those days

A long deep run on a mountain stream. Large boulders, some hidden from the surface, provide holding areas.

when the fish are being difficult. A large, bushy variant or spider-type fly is used and the angler proceeds just a little faster than the current. This causes the fly to skip and bounce, and spectacular are the rises that come to this method. Since the strike is hard and the leader is not on the water, it is a good idea to use a tippet testing at least four pounds. A leader of this size also makes for easier handling of the large, bushy fly.

The method is imitative of the mating and egg-laying flight of the crane fly. Crane flies are usually fairly numerous on meadow streams; their erratic, blundering flight seems to arouse the killer instinct in trout, and this is what makes the method so valuable. It serves to take trout when they are otherwise in the doldrums.

If the lie of a fish under an undercut bank is known with some exactitude, a streamer can be used with telling effect. In this method the angler must use a quiet approach and wait some minutes after getting into position on the bank, downstream of the fish, and three-quarters of a rod length back from the edge. A short, rather heavy leader is needed, as well as a large, bulky streamer or buck-tail.

The cast is more of a dab, and the fly should spat the water. Then it is pulled and skipped about in a small area to induce the fish to think it is a minnow or small fish in trouble.

"Wait for the wind." This is sound advice on meadow streams. When the surface is calm and unruffled, your chances are much better if you wait for a vagrant breeze to ruffle the surface before you make your cast. This applies to both wet and dry presentations and particularly to the streamer method just mentioned.

If the wind is too strong, as it may well be, it is advisable to wait for the wind to drop so that a more accurate cast can be made. Meadow streams at high altitudes are occasionally plagued by strong winds. One must learn not to fight them. Instead, use them.

Use terrestrials during periods when winds are gusty, as the fish are expecting them to be batted into the water at this time. Also, use bushy dry flies, a long, fine leader, and fish with your back to the wind. Let the fly wave and dance as it will. Now and again, it will dip to the surface, and there is apt to be a trout right there waiting for it. Adjust for wind strength by shortening or lengthening line, or by use of a different sized fly.

When it rains, I like to seek out those glassy smooth glides, and canal-like stretches, and fish a half-sunken nymph. This is just a regular, unweighted nymph treated with dry fly oil, and the first 18 inches of the leader is greased. The float is exactly like a dry fly float, but the fish often refuse the full floating fly under such circumstances. The Natant Nylon Nymph is good here also. (See chapter on insects.)

Some of the meadow streams I fish are at elevations in excess of 7000 feet. Consequently, rain sometimes turns to snow. For some reason, which I am totally at a loss to explain, this will produce a sudden spurt of activity if the fish have been lying low. It can't be temperature change (I think) since these streams usually have temperatures in the high 50s and low 60s.

Whatever the reason, such an unseasonable snow stirs up the fish and one gets one of those exceptional days when big trout hit like mad and fight like fury. The harder the snow, the faster the fish hit. I once stood on the bank of the Madison, along a stretch of fine holding water, and took seven trout, from one to three pounds, without moving. It was snowing a veritable blizzard at the time, although it was mid-August. The snow lasted about an hour and a half, and when it quit, so did the fish. Incidentally, this only seems to work on meadow stretches.

Speaking of standing on the bank, I seldom wade meadow streams unless I cannot reach the good lies. I'm not sure whether wading or not wading is the best policy, but I feel too exposed out in the open on calm, unbroken stretches. One might think that a person would be more exposed up on the bank, but by kneeling and/or staying well back, and by wearing dull colored clothing, one can avoid being seen.

In meadow stretches too wide to fish from the bank, the current tends to be slower and the surface smoother. If it is necessary to wade to reach the good lies, the angler must use any form of concealment available. Sometimes the water depth will allow him to kneel, or perhaps he can skulk along the far side of floating weed beds. In cases where neither of these is possible, wait for the wind to ruffle the surface before casting. The swing of an arm, the flash of the rod, can be seen a long way under these conditions.

In wet fly fishing from the bank, whether mountain or meadow stream, the roll cast is a must. I like this cast for several reasons. Developed with a horizontal, rather than vertical, motion, it can be a wind cheater. It keeps fly and leader damp so that they sink

A very fast stretch on a large mountain stream. Pocket water. Flies used here should rely heavily on shape and size.

well. It can be used anywhere there is standing room.

A variation of the roll cast is useful when wading. After the fly has finished its drift, and is downstream of the angler, it is brought to the surface with a gentle pull, which is finished with a swing and cast quartering upstream. In effect, the drift of the fly has replaced the back-cast.

This cast can be made with one's back right against a line of trees, or other obstruction. It also keeps the fly and leader soaked. As the angler wades to a new spot, the fly is allowed to hang at the end of its drift until the desired position is reached, then the fly can be surfaced and flipped to start a new drift. The cast is similar to a tennis backhand.

Mountain stream or meadow stream, there is no substitute for reading the water and getting into just the right position before making the cast. Invariably, there is one spot from which a cast can be made that will allow a dragfree drift and natural presentation. If for some reason one cannot reach this location, a curve cast or snaky line cast must be resorted to. Mountain or meadow, sunlight or shadow, if you present the fly to the fish in a natural manner, you will find him in a taking mood more often than not.

[9]

Western Fly Patterns

In my lifetime of trout fishing, I have tied over 2,000 different patterns of trout flies and have used some 300 of these. I exclude here the hundreds of experimental patterns tied and used (and given to my wife.)

I went through all the usual periods that fishermen—at least fly tiers—do. I was convinced that some of my patterns would revolutionize trout fishing. They never caused a ripple. I underwent periods where I carried as few as six patterns, in a variety of sizes, and other periods where I carried three or four thousand flies in over a hundred patterns and eight or more sizes. After a number of years, I reluctantly recognized two facts: One, there is no such thing as a really revolutionary fly pattern; two, you can overdo the business of fly patterns in both directions.

Buckling down to the unpleasant truth, I then set about studying patterns that had survived for years and were so deeply ingrained in angling that their names were synonomous with trout fishing in this country. Among these are the Quill Gordon, the Cahill, the Coachman, the Grey and Brown Hackles, the Black Gnat and the Hares' Ear.

I can hear you now asking what I'm doing starting off a chapter on Western fly patterns by naming mostly Eastern patterns. Well, a man can learn from his elders, or at least he should. And in this country fly fishing was well developed in the East long before it was in the West.

When I settled down to a serious study of flies of proven worth, the most evident thing about them, which was true to all of them, was simplicity of design. Poking further along this line, it became quickly apparent that a very large percentage of really successful trout flies shared this same characteristic. The most notable stand-out in the opposite direction was the Royal Coachman. It was about this time that I started checking into this fly's reputation, and after a good many years, I've concluded it is a vastly over-rated fly—for catching fish.

With simplicity as the key, I continued my research, now looking toward improving on the old patterns, rather than inventing new ones. Noting how the successful Eastern writer-anglers were beginning to realize that English flies and methods were not too well fitted for conditions in Eastern America, I turned my attention to the West, my chosen country, and began to see what our Western angler-writers had to say. I found considerable dissension among them, to say the least. But as the years went by, the lines of cleavage seemed to be less sharp, and there was more agreement that the West needed its own fly patterns, not just oversized or revamped Eastern patterns.

The first fly patterns truly Western in concept of which I have any knowledge are the Trude flies and their derivatives, which evolved about 1903. These flies were developed for the waters of such rivers as the Snake, Buffalo and Henry's Fork; and off-shoots of them produce well on those streams today.

One of these offshoots is known variously as the Killer Diller, Squirrel Sedge and Snake River Caddis. It is fished mostly dry but is very effective fished just awash or even slightly sunken. It is tied, most generally, in sizes six and eight, 2X long. It has a brown hackle barb tail, yellow body palmered with grizzly, a grey squirrel tail wing laying flat along the body, behind the grizzly shoulder hackle.

There are three other Western patterns similar in design and appearance to the Killer Diller. These are the Vint's Special, Picket Pin, and the Sofa Pillow. Vint's Special was developed by Vint Johnson of West Yellowstone about 1936. It looks like an abbreviated streamer but was designed to be fished as a standard wet. It is almost an exact duplicate of the original Trude, with silk instead of yarn body, and a long shank hook. On the other hand, the Sofa Pillow, which greatly resembles it, was designed to be fished as a dry fly. Both are much used in the Montana,

Unorthodox artificials. Clockwise from top: *Floating Streamer, Matuka, deer-hair hopper, deer-hair cricket;* center: *deer-hair mouse.*

Wyoming, and Idaho areas and account for many big fish. The Picket Pin will serve where either of the others work.

When they appeared, Lee Wulff's series of flies was accepted gladly by Western anglers. It was beefed up, made larger, and a couple of new colors were added. These patterns are still very much in use by Western anglers, somewhat bigger and lustier than Lee intended, but still recognizable. Lee's name still is used, along with the color. They are good standard flies.

The Bi-Fly was developed by Dan Bailey, who also pioneered the Wulff variations. This fly can be fished wet or dry and is an excellent heavy-water fly for big fish.

Flies using hair in their makeup are a good deal more common in the West than in the East and this is a good general way of spotting Western flies. Size is another point of difference. Eastern flies tend to run smaller than size 10, while Western flies tend to run larger. Few Western anglers, however, carry sizes to the length that I and some friends do. With me a size four can be considered average, with 2/0 the largest size and 8 the smallest that I habitually use. Note that I said "use." I carry sizes from 2/0 to 22.

One thing that seems invariably true of Western fly patterns is that they are a far cry from the patterns we inherited from England. Offhand, I cannot recall a single Western pattern that has wings made from the flight feathers of birds. The largest percentage of them, dry flies included, have hair wings; sometimes the whole thing is made of hair, or fur and hair.

Pott's Mite patterns as originally conceived were made entirely from hair of one kind or another, except for a little floss trim. Later models have bodies that are not made from hair, but are otherwise little changed. These flies are unique among Western patterns for their size. They generally run size 10 or smaller.

The Fledermouse, that dandy Western pattern that looks more animal than insect, is a basically sound wet fly which has accounted for some record class fish. Used as is, in places where the gammarus, or socalled fresh water shrimp, is found, it does excellent work. Tied in a darker pattern, it goes well almost anywhere.

It was this fly that led to the evolving, or developing, or whatever you may want to call it, of my own Assam Dragon pattern. It may be interesting to show how this fly developed.

First, I changed the body fur from muskrat to wolverine. I

used it this way a year or two, then changed the squirrel hair for grizzly bear. Another year or so, and the body fur was changed to a mixture of mink, and tan beaver. Another year went by and the bear hair became grouse hackle. Now the pattern was a mink-beaver mixed body and grouse hackle. It was still too light (the body color) to suit me, so I substituted seal fur, then changed the grouse hackle to cock capercailzie, to get a darker fly still. That's how the pattern is made today and it is the first fly I tie on if there are no signs of fish or insect activity to indicate some other pattern is needed.

The Wooly Worm, probably the most sold and most used pattern in the West, is a fly of antiquity. Over 500 years ago it was being used in England, where it was variously called Palmer, Soldier Fly, Pilgrim, Army Worm, and Black Hackle. I have copies of two articles written over a hundred years before Izaak Walton wrote *The Compleat Angler,* and this pattern is described in both.

I first tied this pattern in 1930, for use as a bass fly in the Missouri Ozarks. At that time I had not read much on angling, being only nine years old, and as the fly was unknown in my part of the country, I blithely assumed I had originated the pattern.

I believe that Don Martinez deserves the credit for reestablishing the Wooly Worm as a trout fly. As a Western trout pattern, its authenticity may be a little in doubt, but there is no doubt as to its effectiveness. I would hazard a guess that this one pattern accounts for more worthwhile trout in the Rocky Mountain West than any six other patterns.

The black has been the most popular pattern, with yellow next. However, I prefer a very dark olive to black with black as second choice, brown third, bright orange fourth, and yellow as fifth choice in this fly.

One offshoot, which is sometimes more effective than the original, has grizzly hackle dyed dark orange rather than natural grizzly. I like the olive, black, and brown bodied patterns with this orange hackle. Incidentally, I do not like tinsel or tails on this fly. While I have not experimented enough to be certain, it appears that I get better results without them.

Another fly pattern very popular in the West, although developed elsewhere, is Don Gapen's Muddler Minnow. And now I recall that both this fly and the Western Hopper, a grasshopper imitation, do use the flight feathers of birds, turkeys, for wings. No matter, they are still a far cry from conventional English type patterns.

The Muddler is used both wet and dry, which brings out another point about Western flies. A great many of them can, without any change of design, be used as either a wet or a dry fly, or sometimes as a streamer. The Muddler, Bi-Fly, Buzek's Stone Fly, Vint's Special—all these and more are used as wets, dries, or streamers as suits the caster's fancy. The Mormon Girl with squirrel wing fits in this category also.

The Spruce Fly looks like an abbreviated streamer, but is most often fished as a standard wet. This is almost purely a cutthroat fly in this country, and at certain seasons is very deadly. It is used some for brooktrout, and sees quite a bit of action as a steelhead fly on the Washington and British Columbia coast.

The Montana Nymph and a variation, the Bitch Creek nymph, account for many good fish every year. These flies are quite similar, but the adherents of one swear that the other pattern is not nearly so effective, and vice versa. I have found both to be exceptionally good under certain adverse conditions. After a heavy rain, or when the water is colder than normal, I have used these patterns with success where several more favored ones failed to produce.

Roy Donnelly's big variants come in several colors. All are good. If a single pattern could win me over to dry fly fishing only, this would be it. It has many things in its favor—visibility, floatabilty, ease of casting, ruggedness in use; but its main appeal to me is, that fished in the kind of water for which it was designed, it has never failed to fetch fish of worthwhile size.

We now come to the Goofus Bug, whose origin is somewhat clouded. That it originated in the West is not disputed; it is too typically Western for there to be any doubt of that. Just which part of the West is the question. The weight of evidence seems to indicate it was hatched on the Pacific slope.

Wherever hatched, it has become, in a very short time, a standard dry fly pattern. Part of its appeal lies in its virtual unsinkability; but mostly, this fly is favored by a host of anglers simply because it will take fish just about anytime, anywhere, and anyhow that fish can be taken on the dry fly. I once saw this fly, in a single afternoon, produce three limit catches for three not-too-skillful anglers, and not one of the fish weighed less than three pounds.

Clockwise from top: Pteronarcys californica *nymph, adult, dry caddis, Skunk Hair Caddis (larva).* Center: *Sprite-type fly.*

Shortly after the above was written, I got to chatting with three anglers, members of the North Fork Club, where my friend, Robert Wuthrich has been factotum for a good many years. Robert and his brother Ernest, now deceased, formerly were at the Trude ranch, dating back to about 1910, and they had helped me before with data on old patterns and other matters.

One of these anglers, whose name I unfortunately forgot in the excitement of what he had to say, told me the following history of the Goofus Bug.

In 1938 or 1939, Alexander MacDonald and some friends were fishing the Hat Creek-Rising River area near Burney, California. This one friend was particularly enamored of a recently developed eastern pattern, the Rat Faced McDougall, and the fish were enthusiastic about the fly also—so much so that the angler's supply was soon exhausted. He then began the task of replenishing his supply at night, in the cabin.

He was not an overly skilled fly tier, and was unable to do a good job on the clipped deer hair body; after several attempts he resorted to folding the hair around the hook shank in the manner presently used.

This fellow was kidded quite a bit about this "monstrosity," my new acquaintance said, until the following year, when he accompanied MacDonald up to the Snake River, and in a single day took two trout of over five pounds each on this strange looking bug. Such happenings give a fly instant fame, and the Goofus Bug has been a standby in this area since then. Incidentally, just over the mountains, in Jackson's Hole, the Goofus Bug is known as Humpy, the Wonder Fly.

One thing, perhaps, that led to the adoption of many of our Western fly patterns was the fact that our trout were not as sophisticated as their Eastern brethren. But this isn't really as true as it might seem. We have a little different type of insect, and, if I may indulge in a little Western bragging, they average a few less to the dozen.

This isn't just idle chatter. I've already said that in the West the stone fly is the fly to imitate, and in the West the stone fly reaches a respectable size. *Pteronarcys californica,* a prevalent type throughout the West, is a sizable insect. When ready to hatch from nymph to adult, the nymph will be from 1½ to 2 inches long, and is proportionately broad and thick.

Size doesn't stop with the stone fly. I've fished streams in the West that had cased caddis in them that were from 1 to 1½ inches long, and half as thick as a pencil. I once fished a stream in California where caddis of this size were so abundant that they were crushed underfoot like grapes at a wine harvest.

Other really sizable insect types found in the Western streams are "willow" flies (really the fish fly, Chauliodes species) dobson flies (Corydalis, the underwater form of which, the helgrammite, is two to three inches long), and craneflies—some species of which will span the palm of one's hand. These, with the big stone and caddis flies, form a large portion of the Western trout's diet, and it takes really big artificials to imitate them. The bulk of artificials that I use are imitations of the above, plus dragon fly imitations, which are found everywhere.

A certain lack of delicacy in all fields of endeavor has been the trademark of the Westerner, along with a sometimes violently pursued independence. These attributes have carried over into his fly fishing. It's not only that his flies quite often do not look like flies, in the eyes of a traditionalist, but that he sometimes uses somewhat crude methods of presentation.

I am a Westerner by choice. I would not live anywhere else than where I do if they wrapped the rest of the world up in silver paper and paid me to take it. Yet even I am occasionally abashed at my neighbor's fishing techniques.

Once I was fishing a stretch of the Eel in California. It wasn't steelhead water; it was far above the dam at Van Arsdale, where the Eel is a proper trout stream. Here, sedately fishing my wet fly cast of Gold Ribbed Hares' Ear and dark stone fly, I came upon a lumberjack who was dredging the faster runs and riffles with a number six Grey Hackle Peacock embellished with a good quarter ounce of lead.

I will not tell you how large were the fish he caught, for fear you would not believe me. Suffice to say that one of them was, and still remains, the largest non-steelhead trout I have ever seen taken on a fly.

Perhaps when I used the word "crude" in describing some facets of western fly fishing technique, I made a poor choice of words. Perhaps I should have said "directness," for it is the nature of the Westerner to tackle problems head-on, which may explain why they seem to have fewer problems than other folks. I have found myself that a problem squarely faced tends to disappear.

Along these lines, I was setting around with a bunch of brother anglers several years back, discussing the difficulties of proper dry fly presentation. Among the listening but non-talking anglers was George, who was noted far and wide as a very blunt man, and a first-class fly fisherman. Pretty soon George interrupted our hot little session to remark that all that fooferaw seemed like a long way to go to fool a trout.

"You gotta be subtle !" exclaimed one of the more vigorous talkers. (Maybe it was me.)

" 'Suttle' how ?" George wanted to know.

The eager one launched into a lengthy description of the techniques needed to seduce a trout. When he was finished, there was a long pause. Then George remarked, "Seems to me that being 'suttle' means knowin' how to beat something's brains out with a feather."

Over the passing years, George's remark has come back to me many times, always with renewed impact. In a single sentence he had exposed, for me at least, the prime difference in Eastern and Western angling methods, and perhaps, the difference in flies as well.

There is nothing subtle about a Western fly.

[10]

Unorthodox Artificials

It is a fact of recorded history that the first artificial flies ever to be used were dry flies. Had this not been so, our present-day lures would probably have been called something other than flies.

From what I've been able to deduce, fly fishing disappeared during the dark ages, and when it reappeared during the 14th century, dry fly fishing had gone into obscurity.

During the early periods of its reappearance on the sporting scene, fly fishing was mostly engaged in by moderately wealthy gentlemen, as was all sport fishing. Poorer folks had no time to waste on fancy methods; if they wanted a mess of fish, they secured it in the easiest manner possible.

As a result of this state of affairs, fly fishing became a sport for conservatives. In England, especially, it was much favored by retired military officers and minor nobility, and these were conservative gentlemen indeed. For a couple hundred years, so resistant were these gentlemen to change that no significant changes were made.

Several attempts were made by organized angling groups to establish rules for the fly fishing, and in fact, some associations did this within their own domain: rods could only be so long, lines of so many horse hair links were required, the fly had to be just so.

When angling writers began to write of fly fishing, a number of controversies arose, each writer being backed by his own group of believers. Many angling gentlemen literally came to blows, and all this over so small a thing as whether pig's wool or rabbit fur was the proper body on some fly.

As late as Halford's day, that gentleman was known to remark that he would not use the Coachman fly since it imitated nothing he knew of. Even today, imitation of naturals is pressed to extremes, and there are men who profess to use nothing but exact imitations. That, to put it bluntly, is sheer poppycock. The best fur and feathers ever tied into a trout fly are but a shabby, remote representation of the natural.

It is true that a fly which *simulates* a natural insect will probably lure more fish over a period of time than one that does not. I have no quarrel with that. My quarrel is with those gentlemen of stubborn convictions who insist that only one or two of the insect types upon which trout feed should be imitated. I am also less than impressed by the logic of a man who dreams a five-pound trout has more delicate an appetite than a five-pound bass.

When people started imitating minnows (while still calling them flies), a number of the gentry raised a row to have these interlopers banned. As a result, many worthwhile lures received the stamp of illegitimacy, and developing such lures—flies, if you will—has fallen into disfavor.

I consider it no sin to catch a trout by any sporting method. I use artificials simply because it gives me more pleasure to do so. I have, at one time or other, taken trout on salmon eggs, worms, cheese, beef, minnows, helgramites, grubs, spinners, spoons, plugs, golf tees, yarn, burlap, and you name it. Since I derive more pleasure from fishing with flies, especially flies I have tied myself, I do more of this kind of fishing. But I do not hamper myself in this field by using only stone fly or only mayfly types. If it is taken by trout while living, then I try to simulate it and use it. Over the years, I have found some such lures not worthwhile because they took trout but seldom. And that alone is my reason for not using such so-called imitations.

I took rather quickly to using deer hair mice because my early fly fishing was done on Current River in the Missouri Ozarks, where I was raised, a few miles downstream from Big Springs. I also quickly developed deer hair crickets and grasshoppers. I used deer hair because it would float and because I had lots of it. As a matter of fact, my introduction to fly tying came when I swapped 15 bucktails (deer tails) to a tier named Howard Steen for a couple of lessons and a batch of material. I had meant to sell the bucktails, but fell in love with fly tying instead. It was the best deal I ever made.

When I took to trout fishing, it came naturally to try my deer hair mice, crickets, and grasshoppers; to my not too great surprise, they produced well. They still do.

They work for the plain and simple reason that, in certain areas, they form a regular and sizeable portion of the trout's diet. In the case of larger trout, these also are very desirable tidbits because they represent a good mouthful at a minimum risk.

Plastic or rubber imitations of grasshoppers, crickets, and nymphs leave me colder than Finnegan's feet when they buried him, and I think they impress the trout the same way. These sometimes look very real, but they also look very dead, and given a choice, the trout prefers his food in the living state.

For grasshoppers, I tie the butts of a bunch of deer body hair onto the hook near the eye. Orange silk is then wound over this in a spiral back to the bend and then forward and tied off. The tips of the hair are then folded forward, surrounding the hook shank, and tied off. A piece of cinnamon-spotted turkey wing is folded over the back and tied down. Underneath goes a small wisp of brown bucktail. The head is finished rather large. I use 3X long number six and four hooks. Our grasshoppers aren't this large, but this oversize fly gets results.

Cricket bodies are made the same way, except fatter, and on regular-length number six hooks. I bind the body tightly in the center and lash a few wisps of peacock herl crosswise underneath for legs at the same time. Then I touch the top with a good dose of black liquid shoe polish, and Voila!, a cricket.

As can be seen, I do not go to great lengths to convince the trout that here is the real thing. I've become convinced in latter years that a general impression is better than an overdone imitation. The only reason I have for believing this is that I get better results with the simpler ties.

I have at times used deer hair frogs and crawfish. They don't work as well in the West as in the East, since those creatures are relatively rare in most areas (and completely absent around West Yellowstone) and therefore I no longer use them. However, if I were living in an area where they made up a good portion of the trout's diet, I would use them.

Some years back, I saw a fellow fishing an artificial salamander. This was in the upper reaches of the south fork of the Eel. Small, dark spotted, orange salamanders abounded, and this guy was doing a land office business. I have never seen real or artificial salamanders on a trout stream since, but a friend from Tennessee says he knocks 'em dead every spring with live ones.

For those who would like to try this artificial, nothing could be simpler. Cut a salamander about three inches long out of a chamois car wiper, dip it in a warm—not hot—dye of the desired color, and then spot it with black ink. Slip a hook through the lip and cast away. This fellow I saw had an eight-pounder (a spent steelhead) and two over four, so it catches big ones under the right conditions.

Among somewhat unorthodox minnow imitations, I know of three which are different enough from the usual bucktail-streamer types to warrant separate treatment. One is my own Floating Streamer, which I describe in another chapter. Another is the Matuku Streamer, developed in Australia and New Zealand. They catch plenty of five pounders down there, and ten pounders create no great excitement, so it might be well to examine this fly.

A 3X or 4X long hook is used. Sizes depend on the individual, I prefer number 4 and number 2, in that order. The body is wound with wool of the desired color, right up to the eye. It is quite thick, about two-thirds the thickness of a pencil at the front, tapered somewhat to the rear. A pair of large streamer or nashua feathers are prepared by cutting them three-quarters of an inch longer than the hook shank. Starting at the butt, these feathers are split back toward the tip for a distance equal to the length of the hook shank, and one side is clipped off at this point, leaving the tip intact. The two feathers are matched and faced, set on top of the yarn body, with the tips extending from the bend of the hook. The split portion is then tied on at the bend, and the thread spiraled forward, through the feather fibers which are left standing erect, like a dorsal fin. A little bunch of yarn is fuzzed out under the chin. Jungle cockeye is optional. This is a very minnowlike fly, and it swims well.

I do not know the origin of this last streamer type, which is called the "Maypole" streamer for obvious reasons. The tail is six hackle tips 1½ inches long, tied so as to flare. The body is tinsel garland, called tinsel chenille by some. The wing(?) is eight hackles, extending just past the hook bend, and tied evenly around the shank, so they flare out. Three full turns of long hackle are taken in front of this. Color is up to the individual, but white, badger, and furnace seem most popular. Gold tinsel is used with the furnace; silver with the other two.

The Maypole is strictly a big trout fly. No matter what size hook is used, it comes out a large fly, and, it must be admitted, an effective one. Pulled and twitched through the water it breathes and flares and looks very much alive. It's a killer in rough water, where its flash and action catch the trout's eye, but where there isn't much chance to really look it over. It's a prime high water fly.

Artificial dragon flies are fine lures for really good trout in late summer. Such artificials are as easy to make as they are difficult to cast.

I make the body out of my old favorite deer hair, on a regular-length size 6 fine wire hook. At the bend, I tie on an inch and a half piece of 60-pound test nylon. I wind insect green floss over this down to the bend of the hook and tie off. A bunch of deer hair almost pencil thick is bound on from eye to bend, and the floss is wound over this. Four large grizzly hackles are tied X fashion at the thorax, and a few wisps of peacock crosswise under the thorax at the same time.

This thing is a nightmare to cast, but if it is dropped along the banks of a meadow stream during the middle of a bright sunny day, I'll almost guarantee it will take trout—good ones. It wont take much punishment, but few floating flies will.

For late-evening fishing, a large moth-type dry fly is often a killer. The body is made of clipped deer hair, quite full. Two overlapping guinea breast feathers are tied flat along the back for wings. Three turns of ginger hackle clipped quite short complete the lure. Size four, 2X long is a good choice.

There are still many anglers who turn up their noses at unorthodox artificials. Some of these are skillful enough so that their regular selection of flies take fish most of the time. So, when their flies and methods do not work, they assume nothing will.

As a matter of fact, when fish are taking the ordinary run of flies, unorthodox lures seldom work. When the fish are being difficult, and nothing seems to lure them, this is where the unorthodox lure shines. Most such lures were developed just for such times.

The man who limits himself to a few forms of insect life and a few methods of presentation is going to experience many days where the fish are unwilling. The more strings to your bow, the less chance of being skunked is my philosophy. As stated before, I limit myself to artificials because I enjoy their use more.

A good many years back, a fellow out on the West Coast got caught short, and wrapped some ravelings from a burlap bag around a bait hook. He used this for steelhead and, lo and behold, it proved to be a killer. This is one of the ugliest flies ever conceived by mortal man. The commercial tiers have prettied it up and added some refinements, but they haven't completely succeeded in ruining it.

I'm sure everyone has had the experience of taking fish on a fly that was so chewed up it was coming apart. A new fly of the same pattern wouldn't produce. I've had this experience so often that today a great many of my wet flies come out of the vise looking chewed up. They catch fish.

In lakes, some anglers of my acquaintance use standard bass bugs of subdued coloration. They fish late in the evenings and consider a four-pound trout an average fish. When I fish with these gentlemen, I put on my big Montana Stone dry fly, and we all have a ball. A lot of more conventional anglers look down on us.

But, as George Bundy says, "I laugh every time I reach for the net."

A fellow from Nevada introduced me to the Parachute dry fly. This was a deer hair monstrosity that looked like an exploding sycamore ball. It was called Parachute because it cast like one.

In very rough water, this is a dandy. Before Quake Lake gobbled up that portion of the Madison, it was the best dry fly around for that section. Surprisingly enough, it does good work in less turbulent waters.

It is made of deer body hair tied on the hook any old way, and left untrimmed. It is not neat. It is not meant to be. Even though it does look like a motheaten porcupine it catches trout, and big trout.

The hook point cannot be seen if the fly is tied as per the original. This makes it an excellent fly to fish around floating weed beds. It also causes an occasional missed strike.

Another fellow I know, in effort to avoid missing strikes on this fly, and to make it easier to cast, trims it on the bottom to where the hook point shows. He calls this one Haffa Parachute for obvious reasons.

My Nevada friend didn't know the origin of the fly. He vaguely remembered the fellow who introduced him to it as saying some fellow from California had originated it. It isn't widely known in the Rocky Mountain West, but in the Lake Mead-Havasu-Parker Dam area it enjoys local fame. It should be used more places. It has merit.

I have seen many imitations of ants used, both wet and dry. In some areas, a big, shiny Black Ant is a good wet fly. Other places, it meets with mediocre success. Floating versions of both the black and vinegar, or ginger, ants are excellent. Of course, they work better when there is an infestation of the natural. They have saved the day for me on occasion.

I have seen, but never used, imitations of butterflies. The problem of tying them—and casting them—must be enormous. I have seldom observed trout taking or attempting to take butterflies flitting over the surface of a stream. I do not believe them to be too effective.

This raises a point. Unorthodox flies should not be originated or used just for the sake of using something different. Only if there is sound reason for believing them useful should one bother with them—and this is true of any fly.

A diversified approach to fly fishing has always appealed to me, both from the standpoint of enjoyment and effectiveness. For these reasons, I have probably been more susceptible to the blandishments of the unusual artificial than the average angler. I feel it has added considerably to my enjoyment of the game, and occasionally to my enlightenment.

In passing, I will mention the spinner fly. Here I do not mean a fly tied to be snapped on an Indiana or other type spinner, but one of those flies that has a propeller on the head as part of the fly. Properly designed, this is a good lure, but it is fussy to make and difficult to cast.

I have never had much success with those little metal-backed beetles one sees around. There is a strong possibility that I don't know how to use them, for I have heard of excellent catches being made with them. It would appear that this lure is designed so for weight and glitter, and I can think of better ways to accomplish this.

I have designed, and seen designed by others, floating lures of various materials other than fur, hair, or feathers. I have used sponge, foam rubber, styrofoam plastic, and other materials in making these lures.

I find them not so effective as similar lures of deer hair, clipped or otherwise. They are easier to make, but this is no criterion.

There are hundreds of lures in the casting and spinning field considered somewhat unorthodox for trout fishing. If this were a book on trout fishing rather than fly fishing, I would have lots to say concerning such lures. Since it isn't, I will close with the statement that these lures account for many fine trout each year, and are sporting to use. I no longer use them except on streams or lakes that are literally unfishable with the fly. I think that is as it should be.

〖11〗

The Advanced Fly Fisherman

It is not the number of years spent at the game that distinguishes the advanced angler, nor is it the quality of his tackle and gear. It has nothing to do with the casting skill nor how much he has read on the subject. What then, or who, is an advanced angler?

To paraphrase Robert Burns, advanced angling's a state of mind. An advanced angler, oddly enough, is one who has not arrived. He is still trying to progress. How can we say a man who has not reached his goal, who is still trying to improve, is advanced? We can say it because these very factors have carried the man along until he is, in the angling field, in advance of the herd. He is in the van. He stands head and shoulders above the crowd of ordinary anglers.

His theories may not be new or startling, but he will have them and he will be definite about them. He will have tried and rejected scores of others, and is still willing, even eager, to try new ones, if they are logical and sporting. He clings to the old, if it works, or sometimes (rarely) out of sentiment, but he seeks the new, or at least the better way.

I have known men who have fished for trout for 40 years. They cast beautifully, fish the cast well, are well-read and knowledgeable. People tend to look on these men as advanced anglers. They are not. Except for tackle and gear, they have not added a single new item since the third or fourth year they fished. They have, in effect, stagnated, or stalled at the average angler level.

Their polished technique and long (but not broad) experience gives them a patina of sophistication, but this is the only area where they stand out from the ordinary, run of the mill fishermen. Their knowledge of casting and currents will give them slightly better and more consistent catches than their brethern. They appear advanced in the same way a new model car appears advanced —a glossy finish over the same old design.

Some of these persons—most, in fact—are content. They have accomplished exactly what they set out to. They have no desire to pursue the subject further except in a desultory manner. They are comfortable in their skill and in the knowledge they possess, but they are not advanced anglers. They are, rather, a standard against which the advanced angler can be measured.

Theodore Gordon, in many of his writings, emphasized that a man should not seek to become a better angler simply to catch more fish, but rather to increase his enjoyment.

Others look on fishing as a challenge, and try to increase their knowledge and skill to the point where they can take trout anytime, anywhere. Again, it is not mere numbers these anglers are interested in, but in being able to say that skill, not luck, is what distinguishes an angler.

Peter Hawker of Britain, in his *Instructions to Young Sportsmen,* written in 1814, says that about 90 of 100 fancy themselves anglers, but only one of that hundred really is an angler. Being able to take fish when they are indisposed is what distinguishes an angler, and this is the goal of the advanced angler.

Some men become so skilled in the taking of trout that they seek to equalize matters and increase their sport by going to ultralight tackle, ultrafine tippets, and very small flies.

Arnold Gingrich, a proponent of this kind of angling, calls it 20-20 angling, meaning taking, or attempting to take, trout 20 or more inches long on a size 20 or smaller fly. To accomplish this, he sometimes uses rods of less than five feet, and leaders more than 20 feet in length. Yet he does not disdain to use flies as large as size 4, or longer rods and shorter leaders if the situation demands.

The above points out the fact that theory can only be pushed so far in taking fish, and that the realistic angler yields to realism when necessary. Failure to do so removes an angler from the advanced class.

Several years ago, a well-known member of an old and honored fly fishing club limited himself to two flies for taking trout on club waters. All the members fished the dry fly only. They were extolled by several writers as being very advanced anglers. Implicit in these writings was the fact that these men preferred to take trout on the dry fly or not at all, and that the latter was often the case.

Such persons may very well be advanced *dry fly fishermen,* and it is apparent that this is what they wish to be. They should not, however, be considered advanced anglers or as complete fly fishermen.

In his book *Trout,* Ray Bergman tells of angling with one of the club members just mentioned, and that during the course of the day's fishing, his guest came to realize that there was a decided difference between advanced dry fly fishing, and being an advanced fly fisherman. He recognized also that the difference was not merely due to using more methods, that there was more to being an advanced angler than that.

Many things, all small, make up the difference. Too many persons are prone to call it "luck," "the breaks," implying the difference is due to chance. Others say the difference is due to "desire." Desire, of itself, accomplishes nothing. "He's ambitious," some will say of a person who is in advance of his contemporaries. This is a little closer to the mark. But, again ambition is an empty word unless backed up by action.

The advanced angler must first of all have the desire to advance. He must want to know more about his game, which is neither art, craft, nor science, but a little of all three. He must then apply himself to furthering his knowledge, his physical skills, and his practical experience.

I have known some advanced anglers who did not read on angling; some, in fact, who could not read. These men, for the most part, lived on or near streams which they grew to know intimately through long and constant association, by spending many hours fishing, and studying at the source, so to speak.

Most of us are not so fortunate. Either we are distant from a stream or we must spend most of our waking hours earning a livelihood. But during the evenings, and the long winters, we can read.

Read for pleasure, to be sure. But read also to gain knowledge. I like to think of angling literature as being of two classes, one written primarily for entertainment, the other to teach.

Some writers try to combine both but few succeed. The notable exception I know of is *Taking Larger Trout,* by Larry Koller. (Little, Brown & Company). It is one of the most informative of trout angling books, and one of the most interesting. But it is an exception.

In the field of entertaining angling literature, John Taintor Foote and Henry Williamson write beautifully and well. I recommend their books heartily—for pleasure in reading about your favorite sport. I also like Robert Traver.

For the man who wishes to be well informed on the subject of trout fishing, there are scores of good writers. Just remember, however, we are talking now about the advanced angler, the man who has read most of the books dealing with beginners, and who has served his apprenticeship on the stream. For him, there are surprisingly few books. It is true some authors write of advanced methods or refined methods, but this is usually hidden away among pages of fundamentals, behind endless discussions of curve casts, steeple casts, rod weights, and lengths, fly design, and other basic information which the advanced angler has long ago absorbed.

Koller's *Taking Larger Trout* is one notable exception and is one of three angling books I would not be without. Another is Ray Bergman's *Trout.* I have both editions; the first edition has been read so much, and traveled so far with me, that it barely looks like a book. It now has the shape of an old pillow or some such.

Most valuable, however, from the standpoint of the advanced angler, is Sid Gordon's *How to Fish From Top to Bottom* (The Stackpole Co.). Gordon spends but little time on casting, on knots, paraphernalia and other fundamentals so dear to the heart of the average angling writer. Gordon spends the majority of his time on or in the water, discussing the things, including fish, that live there, why they live there, their place in the scheme of things, and what the results are if they are absent. His book is no lightweight; it is not for the casual reader. It is, in fact, a textbook on vegetation, insects, lakes, streams, and the total effect these have on fishing. You cannot plow through this book in a single night, or, if you are a serious angler, in a single year. It is a textbook, a reference work, to check and recheck against practical experience.

I trust you will understand my emphasis on serious reading for the serious angler. An engineer cannot become an engineer without first studying his subject, then working at it, then working and studying, if he is to become more than a run-of-the-mill engineer.

This is exactly the case with the angler. He must first study his work, then work at it. He becomes an advanced angler when, after absorbing the fundamentals and having some field experience, he recognizes that both reading and practice must be continued in order for him to become fully rounded in his field.

The advanced angler cannot be too hidebound; he must be able to accept new, even radically different, ideas and to absorb the impact of the defeat of some of his pet theories. He must be able to analyze and collate his findings. He must be able, also, to recognize differences in environment, and to gauge the effect these differences may have on angling.

One of the longest held theories dear to the heart of the trout fishing fraternity is that trout are a cold water fish, that they must have icy water to survive. My experiments along this line have disproved this theory and my observations have confirmed this.

Oxygen, trout must have. Water free from deadly pollution they must have. But cold water they do not need to survive. It is true if you take a trout from cold water and immediately place him in warm water, he will die. He will also die if you reverse the experiment.

Water has the property of usually holding more oxygen at lower temperatures. When the temperature of a given body of water rises, it usually gives up oxygen. When it gives up enough oxygen, the trout in that body of water are doomed. But it is suffocation that has killed them, not high temperature. Also, when stream temperatures rise, water levels usually lower, and thus there is less total oxygen available.

There is another compounding effect that higher temperature does have on trout. It increases their metabolic rate, or to put it plainly, it makes them live faster, makes them use more oxygen. Thus a combination of less oxygen in the water, and a greater demand by the fish leads to quick suffocation, which for hundreds of years has been laid to high water temperatures alone.

High temperatures are good for trout. What do I mean by high temperatures? Those in the range of from 75 to 80 degrees F. On a stream in this temperature range, with a plentiful oxygen supply, a two-year-old trout will weigh three times what his brothers and sisters will in a well oxygenated stream that never rises above 55 degrees, food supplies being equal.

Examples proving that trout can not only live, but thrive, in warm water are fairly abundant. The Firehole River in Yellowstone Park runs between 70 and 85 degrees during the fishing season. Silver Creek in Idaho and Hot Creek and Rising River in California are in the same temperature range. All support trout, good trout, many trout, healthy trout. Scale readings of trout taken from these streams compared to those of trout taken from nearby streams of lower temperatures have proven without exception that the trout from the warmer streams reach a much larger size at a younger age.

Part of the growth of warm-water trout is due to the fact that warm-water streams produce more food. Mostly it is due to increased appetite brought on by higher temperatures. Higher stable temperatures, with adequate oxygen, it should be said. When temperatures of a given stream tend to fluctuate into and out of higher levels, the results are less positive, and in some cases harmful.

So ingrained is the "cold water is a must for trout" theory that even when faced with proof that it is not so, most anglers are reluctant to abandon the theory. Even some relatively advanced anglers have argued bitterly that it just ain't so. When faced with facts, scientific findings, and with fish themselves as living proof, they have equivocated.

"Fish from warm water aren't good to eat," they say. "All warm water trout fight poorly," is another gambit. "Warm water causes worms in trout," and other nonsensical mutterings are heard. All are sheer poppy-cock.

So, the anvanced angler must guard against a tendency to stand pat, to take an unmoving position. Even our best-loved and oldest theories are subject to being exploded by scientific exploration, research, or sometimes by just the application of a little logic.

The advanced angler must be especially careful not to base a judgment on too limited findings. All avenues must be explored, unfavorable as well as favorable information must be considered.

As an example of such unfounded reasoning, there is the case of the fisherman who, while taking the temperature of a stream, noticed a hatch starting. He matched the hatch well enough to take his limit, and from that day forward, on whatever stream he happened to be fishing, when the water temperature reached the same point as it had on that magic day in the past, this fisherman tied on the same pattern and size of dry fly he had used then and blithely fished away. He caught few more limits but he was convinced he had the right method.

Even when all available information is considered, the relation between cause and effect can be misinterpreted. Sometimes, after years of success with a particular method, I have discovered, usually from another angler, that my theories as to why the method worked were in error. This, of course, is not nearly so bad as to know all the reasons why a method should work, but to find out in actual practice that it does not. I mention the above information merely to point out that an advanced angler cannot stop analyzing the situation even after achieving apparent success.

Most anglers, it seems, use the trial and error method of finding ways to catch trout. This will work fairly well if one can spend enough time on the stream. As I've said, most of us have a livelihood to earn, and must use shortcuts and spare time if we are to progress as an angler. The trial and error method holds powerful appeal, however, for most of us do not like to think. The trial and error man will catch fish, but he will also draw a lot of blanks, which, somehow, no one seems to remember.

I remember one angler, a clumsy, unfeeling clod of a fisherman who, by constantly telling people he was a great fisherman, eventually convinced many people he was. He played his triumphs up big, but softpedaled his failures.

"Old Harry sure is a great fisherman," a friend commented to me one day.

"What makes you think so?" I inquired.

My friend looked at me in surprise. "Why, everybody knows that!" he exclaimed.

"I don't," I said, "in fact, for the amount of time he spends on the stream, I think he does poorly. You know how many days he fishes each summer. How many big catches, or big fish, have you seen him bring in?" (Harry was not a man to return a fish.)

My friend thought about this a while, then said, grudgingly, "Well, not many, now that you mention it. But he does make some good catches."

"Even a blind pig will find an acorn once in a while," I told him. It wasn't that I wanted to belittle Harry, but rather that I wanted my young friend to use his head. I didn't want him to go through life like Harry, depending on long hours and blind luck to fill the creel. Maybe I was too explicit, because my friend became an advanced angler at a very early age, and if a growing family doesn't take him away from the stream, he may become one of the great ones.

The advanced angler must be sensitive to change. Not only to day to day changes, or seasonal changes, but to changes that occur from one hour to the next during the fishing day.

Once, Joe Johnson and I hit the Madison above the iron bridge early in the morning. Our usual methods didn't produce, and as I've said, our methods are diverse. Joe, the restless one, got the answer about nine o'clock. The fish were lying deep and inactive and wanted a large, bright fly dropped right on their noses. We obliged. By eleven, though, they had quit striking, or so it appeared. Actually, they had just begun. They had moved out of their deep lies and were at holding and feeding stations. When I went back to my big dark flies and natural drift, I was back in business. Two hours later, I was out of business, but Joe had the answer again. The fish were feeding, very discreetly, on top. By three that afternoon, they had moved back into the deep holes, and under undercut banks, and wanted a big bright fly right in the kisser.

It had been an unusual day, unusual enough so that Joe and I sat down before going home, and tried to figure out what caused it. Whether we were right is open to question. But here's how we saw it.

It was late fall. The nights had been very cold, heavy frost was on the grass along the bank until noon. That section of the river was in a curve in the canyon where the sun struck only briefly, at high noon.

When we arrived, the water was cold, the fish were chilled and sluggish. As the water warmed from the influence of the sun on the water in meadows upstream, the fish moved into their normal lies. As the water continued to warm, and the sun struck down into the canyon, some hatching activity started, and the fish fed for a while on top. When the sun went behind the shoulder of the mountain, the chill was sudden, and the fish quickly went back to their deep lies.

Seen in retrospect, it looks as though the pattern should have been obvious to us as the day progressed. It wasn't. But by defining our success after achieving it, we added new dimensions to our angling knowledge and made it more likely that we would recognize the pattern and the causes the next time they appeared.

Thus, it is just as important to know why you catch fish as it is to know why you are not catching them. And to reiterate a point I haven't mentioned for a while, I'm still talking about worthwhile fish, those of a pound or over. It seems plain to me that the more the angler defines success, the more success he will have, and the better he will be able to direct his efforts to the taking of worthwhile fish.

I've mentioned that the advanced angler must show discernment. There are many areas wherein he must display this capability, but if he wishes to concentrate his efforts toward taking worthwhile trout, he must quickly learn to know the techniques, methods, and water types which *do not* appeal to the yearlings. In effect, this is somewhat like breathing. It should come naturally, and no one else can do it for you. You can get artificial respiration in the form of a tip, or having an example called to your attention, but if you don't take hold and apply yourself, you're a dead pigeon.

It is the taking hold, the applying of what he has learned, that distinguishes the advanced angler. It is what distinguishes all men who advance in their fields.

The advanced angler never stops advancing; he continues to progress. The advanced angler is therefore always the advancing angler.

[12]

Random Thoughts

The old argument, the fly versus the method, has been going on for as many years as artificial flies have been in use. By method, fishing wet or dry is not meant, but rather, the exact method of presenting or fishing the fly. I have often stated my position that I believe the natural drift with the fly not over six inches off the bottom to be the most productive day in, day out. But I have never regarded it as the only method. Rather, it is the basic one, the point from which I always start, unless there is definite, visible, sign of feeding activity.

The trout observed feeding is usually readily caught, and the choice of fly and/or method usually indicated at once.

It is the non-feeding trout that is hardest to entice and since this is usually the condition that prevails, it is the one which will require the most attention to the proper selection of fly and method.

Those old professors who pooh-pooh the fly and hawk the method overlook one big point in the matter of choosing the "right" fly. Confidence in his choice is at least 50 percent of the reason for an angler's success. He who does not have confidence in his chosen lure will catch few fish. This is why a "favorite" fly tends to develop. A man has good success with a certain fly, and continues to fish it more and with more confidence. The Royal Coachman is the best example of this. Some years back a survey indicated this fly outsold all others in shops throughout the country. Did this prove that the Royal outproduced other flies? A survey along that line conducted by fish and game departments of several states indicated that it did—until one alert biologist-statistician took the time to reduce the overall totals to fish-per-hour average. The Royal Coachman then dropped completely out of the first ten in terms of efficiency. More of them used more hours accounted for more fish, but the fish-per-hour list was headed by flies like the Cahill, Leadwing Coachman, Gordon, and Grey and Brown Hackles.

Confidence in a fly can be misplaced. I once found myself continuing to fish the Black Wooly Worm and Assam Dragon after five hours and several changes of method produced no strikes. Finally, I made a "desperation" change to a small, brown-bodied, black-hackled fly. The first cast into a run I had just fished fruitlessly with the other flies produced a 1¼-pound rainbow, the third found me latched onto a big shouldered brown I estimated at six to seven pounds, which I lost through unusual circumstances. I was backing up to beach the nearly tired out fish when the felt sole came off my right wader foot and I fell down, snapping the leader.

Generally speaking, I will not change flies—nor stretches of water—until I have given both a thorough try with several methods of presentation. I do not consider a hundred casts over a stretch of water 25 by 50 feet in size to be excessive for one method of presentation. Four or five changes of presentation result in as many hundred casts before I am ready to change flies or move on. I am not the traveling type of angler, preferring to spend my time and energy on water I know contains fish rather than race from stretch to stretch looking for a trout on the feed.

*   *   *

The greatest asset in trout fishing, in my opinion, is not to be found in the tackle nor gear, but in the presence of an eager and experienced companion. Sharing a pleasure more than doubles it, but I am not thinking primarily of that aspect. Instead, I call to mind how many times the problem of the day was resolved by one angler and passed onto the other, and the many times when a careful discussion of flies, water, and method suddenly produced the clue that led to solving a problem which until then had appeared unsolvable.

Ideally, angling companions should be of different temperaments. This will provide the greatest probablity of diverse approaches, and seems to produce excellent harmony.

Some of the happiest and most productive angling days I've ever spent were in the company of Joe Johnson. Joe is young enough to be my son; he is eager, enthusiastic, mercurial, a fly changer, and a bank runner. He will fish three miles of both banks of a stream while I am covering one-third that distance of one bank. He changes flies half a dozen times an hour.

I plod along, casting much, moving little, methodically covering each spot or stretch of holding water thoroughly. I favor the deep fly, naturally drifting. Joe prefers the steady, twitching retrieve about mid-water. His choice of flies is drastically different. In a morning's fishing, we will, between us, have covered a variety of water with a variety of flies and methods. When the problem is solved, as it usually is, a whoop brings the other to share the secret. I can only recall one day when we were skunked, and there were no reports coming into the West Yellowstone shops that day of any decent catches in the area.

Looking back over the highly successful angling partners I have known, it seems that the most successful were those of opposite temperaments. Chuck Augustine and Nick Marzetta of the Pacific Coast are of this type and are at the top of my list of best fishermen I could name. Chuck is reserved, placid, methodical. Nick is the Buzz Fazio of the trout fishermen, bubbling, effervescent, full of zest. They stand out in my mind as the most accomplished pair of anglers I know, and about the happiest, although the outsider is apt to be misled by their constant ridiculing of each other's tactics and abilities.

Altogether, angling is not a sport for crowds. But it is the most companionable of sports and the one that lends itself most to mutual aid and instruction. No angler will meet another without inquiring "what luck?" and if the answer is "good!", without asking about the fly or method which produced the happy results.

* * *

Sweetest of all angling fruits, in my book, is that gathered while sitting around the fire or on the porch after the day's fishing is ended, with a number of similarly inclined nuts, with a cold beer or a tall drink, discussing the day's developments. No scientific seminar is more rewarding, no social gathering more satisfying, and even if today was bad, there's always the hope of tomorrow.

When I was much younger and much less experienced, it seemed to me I learned as much during these all-too-rare sessions as I did in a week's fishing. These were serious anglers I hung around, no casual chit-chat filled their evenings. They probed each other's minds; all were intent on learning from each other the methods and secrets they themselves had not learned or tried. Little or no time was spent on discussing what happened after the fish struck, but everyone listened intently to every word of what was done to induce the fish to strike.

They were well acquainted with Hewitt and La Branche, with Bergman and Knight and other writers. However, they did not hesitate to disagree with even a favored writer if their experiences proved his theories wrong, or as was more often true, unworkable on their particular streams.

The best example of this that I remember involved an angler with extensive experience on the Neversink and Beaverkill, who had also fished the Madison, the Gunnison, the Snake, and many streams on the Pacific slope and in Europe; another who had extensive experience only on the Gunnison; one who had fished only the Pacific slope, and another who had fished throughout Wyoming, Montana, Idaho, as well as Scotland and Norway.

They were discussing a theory formulated by a well-known and respected Eastern angler-writer.

"That theory won't work on the Gunnison," said the Gunnison man positively. The Pacific Slope man allowed it wouldn't work in his area either. The Northwest man said it was unworkable on Northwest streams but he had observed it used successfully in Scotland.

The Neversink-Beaverkill angler nodded. "You're all right," he declared "I've seen it used on all the streams and places we've mentioned. The only places I've known it to work are on the Beaverkill, the Neversink, and some streams in Scotland."

The point to be made here is that a method may be sure-fire on one stream or in one area, but be useless elsewhere. In certain lakes in California, process cheese produces limit catches of fine fish, while it is worthless in most other lakes in the state. Such examples are found laced throughout the weave of angling experience.

The advanced, or advancing angler, then, must learn to discriminate, to select those theories and practices that work for him or work on his streams, and to reject those that do not, no matter how successful they may have been elsewhere.

*   *   *

I once recall seeing a fellow from New York State, an excellent angler, fishing the Madison. His tackle and technique were top quality, but he was catching nothing. I fished down three long runs behind him. In the last one he hooked a small brown about seven inches long. I had landed several over twice that length. When I reached the bottom of the last run, he was waiting for me.

"All right," he said genially, "I'm doing something wrong. What is it?"

"Maybe it's that you're not doing something right," I replied, "let me see your fly."

"You're not one of those the-fly-is-all-that-counts fellows!" he protested. "I've caught tons of trout on this cast, so it can't be the flies."

But it was. He was using three sparse, lightly tied, pale colored, number 12 flies. I passed him my cast, with its heavy bodied, dark, number 4 tail fly and a darker number 6 dropper.

"This is heavy water, and deeper than it looks," I told him, "it may be that the fish do not see your flies, or if so, that they will not come up to them. My flies are big and dark enough to be seen, and are weighted to get them down in this current."

He wagged his head over the flies I presented him, but tied them on. As I said, his technique was good. In a few casts he was into a good fish, and after that we fished along with honors about even.

The next year I encountered him rigging up on the bluff above Hole Number 1 on the Madison in the Park.

"Hi," he greeted me as though it had been yesterday when we parted, "those flies you gave me didn't do a thing back East. I tied up a bunch thinking to make a killing, but had to give up on 'em."

"You try 'em real early in the spring?" I asked, "or under high water conditions?" He confessed he hadn't.

"But, I see what you mean," he said, "flies are designed for certain conditions. Those you gave me were more for depth and faster current than is normal on the streams I fish. I've got the picture now. Match the conditions, that's the idea." That's the idea.

*　　*　　*

Speaking of matching conditions, the dry fly man will tell you that's what he does. He does, when it suits his prearranged notions. When there's a rise on he fishes the rise and when there's a hatch on he matches the hatch. He's fishing the conditions—conditions that exist maybe 10 percent of the time. The rest of the time he's doing what he accuses the wet fly man of—chucking it and chancing it.

I put this to a man I knew many years ago, a trout fisherman with over fifty years' experience, and a dry fly purist. He agreed that it was a true picture.

"But," he said, condescendingly, "there is nothing else left for the dry fly man."

"I saw you fish down through the meadows just now," I said. "It's true no fish rose ahead of you and there was no hatch on. But some fish did rise behind you."

"They did?" he said in surprise. "To what?"

"To grasshoppers you scared out of the grass," I replied.

He raised his brows. "I wouldn't fish with grasshoppers," he said stiffly.

"Would you fish with a live caddis fly?" I asked.

"You know I wouldn't," was his firm reply.

"But you have an imitation caddis on your leader," I said softly.

He frowned at the fly, glanced at me, then back at the fly.

"I see," he nodded slowly, "you're saying an artificial grasshopper would have matched the existing conditions and done the job. You're right, of course. I don't have any but I'll get some and what's more, when conditions are right, I'll use them." And he did.

However, the dry fly man restricts himself unnecessarily if he stops with stream imitations and grasshoppers. There are many land borne insects worth the dry fly man's time to imitate. Because trout are accustomed to their random appearance on the stream, they are taken unsuspiciously by the fish almost any time, and this is especially true if no hatch is on. Among those imitations that have filled the dry fly man's creel when no hatch was on are Japanese beetles, crickets, moths, dragon flies, ichneumon flies, ants, hornets, horse flies, blue bottle flies, jassids, leaf hoppers and numerous others. In size they range from size 22 to 2 and if the dry fly man wants to throw delicacy to the winds, he can go in for deer hair imitations of frogs and mice. If I were restricted to fishing on the surface exclusively, 90 percent of my lures would be imitations of the above, to include the last two.

Several years back, a huge old cannibal brown lived in a hole in the bank on the Firehole River in Biscuit Basin. I had seen him once or twice as I sneaked along in search of rises. His dog-like head and hooked lower jaw marked him as a fish long past his prime, and better removed from the stream.

I was something of a dry fly purist where the Firehole was concerned, but the old boy would have none of my floaters, including a deer hair mouse.

I reluctantly switched over to streamers and bucktails, again without results. He made a couple of desultory snaps at a huge (No. 2) Black Ghost Marabou, but his heart wasn't in it.

I recollected a lure that I had concocted back in the Ozarks in my youth for the taking of pickerel when they were in the summer doldrums. For want of a better title I had called it a Floating Streamer, and had forgotten it when I left the region.

I whipped up one on a 6X long, 2X fine wire gold plated number 2/0 hook. The body was the tip of a large goose quill cut to the right length, scraped thin and slipped over the eye of the hook, pointed end rearward. A small piece of cork was glued into the front of the quill, a thin bunch of bucktail was tied on top, the head was wound with black thread and varnished. A large transfer eye adorned the head. The body was spotted with red fingernail polish.

I slapped this down on the surface near the old boy's lair one fine sunny morning, jerking and twitching it, making it act as much like a dying minnow as I knew how. It must have been a good job, the old boy rushed out from under the bank and engulfed the lure so voraciously that it came out through his gills and hooked him in the side. My tackle wasn't built for this, but even so I might have landed him had not his teeth eventually cut the leader. Later a ranger told me privately that the fish had been removed from the stream by other means. He didn't amplify.

This lure was and is a most effective top water lure for large trout, especially browns. I caught a four-pounder with it at Hole #3 on the Madison one day when it was snowing so hard I couldn't see the lure. Trout smash this lure as they do no other I know; I've had several, like the big cannibal, that hit it so hard it came out the gills and hooked in the side. I once hooked in this manner a two-pound rainbow, in fast water. I had 60 feet of line out and thought I had a 10-pounder before landing him.

I also make a sunken imitation similar to this lure, but it has never been any more successful than a regular streamer.

*   *   *

Several years back, when I was a seasonal visitor to the Yellowstone area instead of living here, I used to hear rumors about a fisherman known to the fraternity as "Old Monotone." I assumed it was because this gentleman hummed or crooned to himself as he fished, a rather common trait.

When fishermen gathered at the end of the day to quench their thirst, and tell their bland lies, it was common to hear someone say "Saw Old Monotone today." Or, "Almost fell over Old Monotone again," the remarks would go. This fellow appeared to fish the same streams and areas that I did at the time—that is, the golden meadows of the Firehole and Madison—but somehow, I never ran into him.

One fall, my wife raised such a fuss about the condition of my fishing clothing that I bought a new sage-green fly-fishing jacket and a matching hat to replace the tannish jacket and hat that I had been wearing for umpteen years.

Two falls later, I was having an Old Fashioned in the bar of the Totem in West Yellowstone and talking to my friend Perry, the bartender. It had been a blustery cold day with wet snow, and the gang was quitting early. I was soon joined at the bar by two fishermen in full regalia—jackets, waders, nets, etc. They were dressed identically, except one had flies on the band of his hat, the other did not. They decided my Old Fashioned looked good and ordered a couple.

"Seen Old Monotone lately?" said Flies-on-his hat to the other fellow.

"No," said No-flies thoughtfully. "I used to stumble over him all the time, but I haven't seen him for a couple of years now."

"Me either," said Flies. "Wonder if he passed on or something."

Perry apparently knew the two fishermen well, since he had addressed them by name. This emboldened me to ask a question.

"Who is this 'Old Monotone'? I've been hearing about him for years but I've never seen him."

"Well," replied Flies, "he used to fish the Firehole and Madison meadows all the time in the fall. Wore waders, jacket, and hat the same color as the grass. He knelt down a lot, didn't move anymore than a stump, and you'd almost fall over him before you saw him."

"What's so unusual about that?" I asked. "I camouflage myself when I fish, and so do most fellows."

"Sure," said No-Flies, "but this guy was some kind of a nut or something. He painted his rod ferrules brown, rubbed the shine off his rods and even wore a nylon stocking over his face."

It was at this point in the conversation that I realized the reason I had never met "Old Monotone." The man they were talking about was me.

I still do all those things when I fish the dry fly for large trout. I don't go to quite the extremes I used to, but I still keep the ferrules brown, the gloss rubbed off the rods, and if I wear sun glasses, I wear a stocking or headnet over my face. And if the weather is very calm, the water very clear, and the fish very wary, I rub dirt on my hands.

I've hunted crows and ducks long enough to know that exposed hands and face ruin any attempt to camouflage the rest of the body. Also, who has not seen the shine from ferrules, or the flash from a rod of an angler casting far enough away to be otherwise indiscernible.

Fishing faster, deeper runs, or broken water, with the wet fly, some of the above may be superfluous, but not always. I've seen far too many big trout put to flight by the mere appearance of a white shirt or other light-reflecting outer garment. In most cases, it is the flash of reflected light and not the color that frightens the fish. Mirror-type sun glasses are the worst offenders of this sort, but any kind of glasses are bad enough.

*   *   *

There are times when the old methods, the tested, the tried and true methods, do not produce. It is during these periods that I try the unusual dry fly techniques, and twitching, skittering, and jerking the wet fly. Sometimes if these fail, I switch to unusual or outlandish flies. Sadly, there seems to be periods when these don't work either.

For these not-too-frequent occasions, I have some flies that I do not use until I have run the gamut of other flies and methods. Most every good fisherman I know keeps a supply of such flies. Some call them "the desperation box," others "the last resort flies." I call my flies for this predicament "Market fishing flies," since I got the idea from reading about English market fishermen of 200 years ago.

I use three different types of flies, called Striders, Sprites, and Invisibles. Striders are tied in one size, number 6, 2X long. They are made in eight body colors with two kinds of hackle, making a total of 16 patterns of this type fly. The body colors are black, cinnamon, yellow, orange, red, green, olive and blue, tied long and thin, and closely ribbed with fine gold wire. Hackles are either grouse, or wood duck flank, tied sparse and long.

I never fish these wet flies in other than three fly casts, all three different in body color. Two methods of presentation are used.

In stiller waters, or medium deep runs, I use the natural drift, casting up and across. At the end of the drift the flies are retrieved in foot-long, slow pulls, and allowed to drop back six inches or so after alternate pulls. This method has produced more doubles than any other cast and method I have ever used. It takes fish from eight inches to four or five pounds.

The second method requires a short cast. It is used in the faster riffles and shallower runs. The flies are cast directly across, and a hand and rod retrieve started immediately, with the rod tip being twitched and shaken throughout the retrieve. The flies are kept constantly moving across the current, in the surface film, sometimes in the air.

Sprites are tied in badger, grizzly, and furnace, on 2X short, goldplated number 12 and 14 hooks. No body is wound, just two turns of the longest, softest hackle available. In the badger and furnace colors, a very narrow black center is preferable.

I've had best luck with these in deep, quiet pools, and deep eddies. One July Fourth, after fishing from daylight until four in the afternoon without a strike, I switched over to a Sprite, which I always fish singly. The color was grizzly. I had been fishing the South Fork of the Yuba, in the canyon below the Downieville Highway.

Below the canyon, the river drops over a low fall, encounters the input of a small, spring-fed feeder, recoils off a house-sized boulder, and forms a deep, fast-moving eddy.

I dropped the Sprite into the far side of the eddy on the end of a 12 foot, 3X leader. It made about three full circuits of the eddy, getting down about six feet or so. Then there came a smashing strike, and the line went slack. I retrieved to find the fly gone. I shortened the leader to 2X by removing a tippet, tied on another Sprite, and repeated the performance, including the loss of the fly.

Down to 1X went the leader, and on went another Sprite, a badger this time. Three or four circuits of the eddy, and bang! The same thing happened.

I put on a new leader, one testing a full four pounds, another Sprite, and down I went after them again. Same result, except I hooked this fish and played it until it got into the fast water below the eddy and took off for the Pacific. I was fishing from the top of the boulder and couldn't follow, and when the fish hit the end of the line, the leader parted with a crack like a rifle shot.

About this time my dog showed up, and began running out on the rock, then back up the river bank, looking back at me. He repeated this performance several times before I got the message.

I followed him back into the canyon, where my wife, her brother, and his wife had been fishing. My brother-in-law had suffered a heat stroke, and my wife and his were unable to get him to the car. My wife had sent the dog to fetch me, which he had done the best way he knew how. Incidentally, the last fish was a rainbow of five or six pounds. The dog was a Border Collie—Mexican Shepherd cross.

Sprite flies, fished in the same type locations during tough conditions, frequently produce excellent results. I do not use them during periods of normal fishing, because at these times, they attract far too many six- to ten-inch fish.

I originated my Invisible flies to cope with a particular condition on a particular stream. The Firehole, in the evening, will sometimes come alive with what appears to be an authentic dry fly rise, but with no flies in evidence. I thought for years that these fish were nymphing, but a nymph didn't work either. The answer came by accident.

I had designed a dry fly for this stream, with thin black wool body, badger hackle, and lemon woodduck wing. I used it in sizes 16 and 18, but with indifferent results.

One evening, while casting this fly to one of these "Nuisance" rises, I became careless and let my back cast drop. The fly snagged in the tall grass behind me.

By this time, I was in a snit from casting for an hour over rising trout without a strike. I snatched the rod forward, not caring whether I broke the tip, or lost the fly.

As luck would have it, I did neither. Instead, I stripped the hackle from the size 18 fly, and thereby opened the door. The fly shot forward, straightened the line, recoiled, and dropped well out, with a nice amount of slack in the line.

I recovered the slack and started to pick up the fly, only to discover I had a fish on. After I landed it, I examined the fly. All that remained was the body and a wisp of wing. But I took a dozen good fish on it before darkness set in.

I have not made a single change in the pattern since. I have found that when fish are rising as described, many, many casts are often necessary to raise one. For a long time, many years, in fact, I never knew the reason. Then, in 1961 I read Vincent Marinaro's book, *A Modern Dry Fly Code* (G. P. Putnam's & Sons.) In his chapter entitled "Fishing the Dry Fly on Quiet Waters," Marinaro relates of finding, by accident, that the waters of the Letort were covered with thousands of minute insects, size 18 to 24 and smaller, and that those minutae were responsible for some baffling rises during which he had been unable to catch a fish. From this experience, he and Charlie Fox developed the jassid and other tiny flies.

After I read Marinaro's book, I took a closer look at the water the next time a "nuisance" rise was on. Sure enough, the water was covered with tiny, almost invisible insects. Some were mayflies, dark blue, about size 22; some were caddis, beige colored about size 18; there also were some tiny ant-like flies present.

Shortly after I read the book, I spent some time in the hospital. My nurse was the daughter of a Pennsylvania fly fisherman who fished the very waters Marinaro wrote about. Her father sent me some flies, among which was an odd white deer hair pattern called "Bread Crumb," and a size 18 cinnamon bodied fly with just a wisp of wing and no hackle.

Now I use the two Invisible flies together, about 18 inches apart. Usually, I put the black on the end, and the cinnamon on a fine dropper above it. There are times when they produce when absolutely nothing else will. Always, this is when the "Nuisance" rise is on.

*   *   *

When the fishing is absolutely dead, and no method works,

the fish can sometimes be stirred into striking by inducing insect activity. Go to the tail of a rapid or a fast run. Turn over several dozen rocks in a line across the stream. This will expose a number of nymphs to the current, and some of them will be swept downstream to lies below.

The appearance of live, free-floating or swimming nymphs will quite often arouse the trout and start them feeding. Then the angler can drop down, quietly get into position, and start casting. Success will usually be his.

One word of caution: Indiscriminate tumbling or rolling of rocks may disrupt the stream flow, and ruin some of the closer lies below. Use care when turning rocks so as to avoid this, or skip the method altogether.

*   *   *

I have found binoculars a great aid in studying both trout and stream insects. When a trout is rising across the stream from me, to some insect which I cannot see, binoculars will often bring the fish and insect literally within arm's reach, where they can be studied leisurely, and without frightening the fish.

Also, the use of binoculars does away with dashing after a member of the prevalent hatch in order to identify same. Just focus on the nearest lit specimen and you'll find that in most cases you can study it much better than a captured one.

I find lightweight 6 x 30 binoculars entirely adequate for this kind of work. Inexpensive binoculars are all right, since they are used at short range, and are not used steadily for long periods as in hunting. Incidentally, I buy cheap polaroid plastic sunglasses, cut circles out of the lenses, and tape them over the objectives of the binocs. They are a great help in studying fish and insects underwater.

*   *   *

I do not believe that studying the stomach contents of trout I have caught has been of much help in catching more or larger trout on that particular day. There are several reasons for this belief.

First, if I have caught a trout to study, I'm already on the right track. Second, when I open the trout I usually find a mixed bag; that is, a combination of different insect forms, or sometimes minnows, frogs, crawfish, other trout, and so forth. Third, if the contents are fresh and undigested, the trout has just gone on the feed. Logic has already told me this.

Over the long run, I have learned much from such studies, but I cannot recall a single instance where studying the stomach contents of a trout I have caught has aided me solving the immediate problem.

I recall one instance among many, which demonstrates my point perfectly. Another angler and I were fishing the Madison in the vicinity of Hutchins. For three hours, we cast without results. During this period, my friend changed flies several times. I stayed with my two-fly cast.

About ten o'clock I took the first fish, of about 1½ pounds, immediately after I landed it, my friend came racing up.

"Open it up," he said gleefully, "now we'll find what they're feeding on."

The stomach of the fish held only three nymphs, all large stone fly nymphs, all still alive. Obviously, the fish had just commenced to feed.

"Good," said my friend, "put on a stone fly nymph and we'll kill them."

"What do you think I caught him on?" I queried.

He stared. "You caught him on a stone fly nymph? Why, I used one for an hour and never got a strike."

"I used it for three hours and never got a strike," I replied, "the fish have just started to feed."

To this day, my friend is convinced that we solved the problem by opening the fish, when in fact the problem was solved when the fish was hooked.

*   *   *

I once read an article by that fine Western angler-writer, Ted Trueblood, entitled "Skip the Middle." It's excellent advice, because in streams trout do not feed in midwater, except perhaps one percent of the time.

When a trout is in midwater, he is there because he can see either the surface or the stream bed better. If he hits a nymph or fly at that level, it's because nymphs are rising to the surface to hatch, and that happens to be the level where he overtook it. If such is the case, a well-chosen fly drifted anywhere between the surface film and the stream bed will take fish. As the hatch progresses, the trout will move one way or the other; that is, they will commence to take the majority of the nymphs as they break loose from the bottom, or as they reach the top.

Which way they elect to go depends on a number of factors, but basically it hinges on simple greed. The trout will go where he can catch the most nymphs or flies in the shortest period.

*   *   *

The evolution of artificial flies has always had a strong facination for me. One result is that my angling library includes many books that are more about flies than they are about fishing. I could not be parted from them for all the rice in China.

It is interesting to note that sometimes, in the course of years, a change will occur in the dressing of the fly, but not in the name. And quite often, the reverse is true.

The oldest fly of which there is any written record, goes back to the third century A.D. The fly was called *Hippourus* (in Greek.) When next this fly appears in angling literature, it is nameless; but its description was identical to the Greek *Hippourus*.

Later on, this fly became the Red Heckle, then the Red Hackle, and now is known throughout America as the Brown Hackle, Red Body.

There are many thousands of fly patterns which at one time or another have been pictured or described in angling literature. A great many flies, though quite different, have had the same names. Mostly, this wasn't too important, but now and then, a fly will become a standout, but much confusion exists because there is another fly of the same name.

A case in point is the Cahill. In Mary Marbury's *Favorite Flies and Their Histories,* the Cahill is pictured and its origin ascribed to Ireland. In H. H. Smedley's *Fly Patterns and their Origins,* the author states the fly was originated by an American, Dan Cahill.

Both of these authors are correct. They are just talking about two totally different, completely dissimilar flies. Marbury's Cahill has a yellow body ribbed with silver, green hackle, and a golden pheasant tippet wing and tail. Smedley's Cahill has a body of dun dubbing, brown hackle, and lemon-speckled woodduck wing and tail.

Also, in Marbury's book, two identical flies were called by different names, the fly known as a Parker in the East was quite famous in the West as the Klamath. It is still a good steelhead fly in the Oregon-Washington areas.

Perhaps, when it comes to taking fish, the above goings on do not matter, but, on the other hand, the serious angler may now and then find himself handicapped by this kind of confusion.

Suppose, before going into a certain area to fish, you ask a friend who has fished that section for a list of flies, then send that list to your tier to have the flies made up. Then, when it is too late, you find your friend and the tier were not of the same mind as to the flies' dressing. This can, and has, spoiled many a trip.

The thing to do, of course, is to obtain the details of the dressing and send those to your tier, rather than the names of the flies you want.

A good many years ago, I was going into a rather remote area to fish. I asked a friend who had fished there to recommend some flies. He said he had only needed one pattern for that region, the Whirling Blue Dun. I asked him to describe the pattern so I could make up the flies.

"Just make the standard pattern," he replied.

I pressed him for details, and was amazed when he described exactly our old friend, the Cahill.

Once, an angler from the East was coming out to spend a month in the Sierra. Having no flies for this region, he got recommendations from several friends. One of them advised him not to have the flies made in the East, as they might prove different. This seemed sound, so the angler ordered the flies, by name, from an outfit in San Francisco. When they came, his friends were astonished. Only two of the patterns received, of a half dozen ordered, were of the design recommended. So much for the names of flies.

It can happen to anyone. Once, Jack Warren advised me to take plenty of the fly pattern called "Rock Worm" on a trip into the backwoods. One of my catalogues had a Rock Worm pattern in it, and I whipped up a bunch. They looked great.

Well, they didn't work, and when I returned, I jumped Jack— rest his soul, he has since departed—about it. Of course, his Rock Worm pattern had been nothing like mine. Nowadays, when someone recommends a fly pattern to me, brother, I get a description. Not only that, but if there's time, I tie up a couple and show the guy. Invariably, I find that when he said a red tail, he meant cardinal, not Rhode Island. If he said barred woodcuck wing, he meant lemon, not black and white.

Even the types of fly themselves are subject to foulup. A nymph to some people is any wingless wet fly, while others call this "grub"; still others call it a hackle, while there are those who refer to it as "buzz" or buzz tied.

Long hackled, sparsely tied wet flies are called variously striders, spiders, pool hackle, and crickets. A streamer by one fellow's definition may be any long wet fly, and a bucktail may be made of bear hair, raccoon tail, monga, kip, impalla, or any other hair or tail. In casual talk, this lack of precision of terms is of no importance. But it is of first magnitude to the man who wishes to duplicate a fly of which he only knows the name.

*   *   *

Somewhat apropos to the above is the confusion engendered by the names of streams or lakes. For instance, within 50 miles of West Yellowstone are four Rock Creeks, three Hell Roaring Creeks, several Sheep Creeks, three Swan Lakes, several Fish Creeks and Fish Lakes. If a fellow just sets out for one of these places, he may find the right place but the odds are against it. What to do? Either get directions from the fellow who told you about the fishing or ask him to point it out to you on the map.

Speaking of maps, good fishing maps are wort! their weight in gold. The best ones I have found are U.S.G.S. quindrangle maps. Most of these are available in the 15 minute series, at a scale of about 1 mile to the inch, but in some areas 7½ minute series are available. This represents a scale of about 1 mile to 2 inches. These maps are available from the U.S. Geological Survey, Denver 25, Colorado, or Washington 25, D.C. at 30 cents each. It is best to order a state index which is free, first, so that you will be able to see exactly what maps are available.

[13]

Thoughts on Tackle and Gear

By the time a man begins to approach the advanced stage of angling, it's a pretty safe bet that he has accumulated a vast amount of tackle and gear, some of which is worthless or nearly so. It's also a pretty safe bet that, worthless or not, he cannot be parted from it except in dire circumstances, or in the course of fishing.

When I went into service in War II, I gave away all my fishing and hunting equipment. When the war was over, and I started to recoup, much of the stuff that could be purchased was of inferior quality, and even that was scarce. Yet I look back on that time somewhat gratefully: first, because not having any tackle or gear at all makes one realize how important it is; second, but no less important, owning poor and inferior equipment gives one a finer sense of judgment and appreciation of better equipment.

A man who has never owned anything but good rods, reels, lines, and the rest, simply cannot know what a wide gap exists between average fly fishing equipment and very good fly fishing equipment. The gap between very good and the best is almost nonexistent as far as performance is concerned. Finer fittings, deluxe finish, and fancy work is about all that distinguishes the best from the very good.

I purchased 13 fly rods in the period between 1946 and 1952, each one of a little better quality than the last. This progressive moving up in quality taught me better than any other method the differences in quality that were important, and those that were not.

Anyone who has owned fishing gear for any length of time is bound to have some set ideas about his likes and dislikes. Nearly all of us, though, still like to prowl through the tackle shops and catalogs on the lookout for items that suit us a little better.

I have read everything about angling I could lay my hands on for 40 years. During that time I've become more and more amused at the way the average angling writer pussyfoots through the jungle of brand names without once mentioning them. Some go to ridiculous lengths to avoid doing so.

The reason for this eludes me, especially the case of angling editors of outdoor magazines. I notice the gun editors suffer no such inhibitions. In the same issue of a magazine you will find such diverse approaches as these: GUN EDITOR: "The rifle was a model 70 Winchester equipped with a 4X Bear Cub scope on Buehler mounts. I was using 48 grains of Du Pont 4895 behind 130 grain Sierra soft points, touched off with Western primers."

FISHING EDITOR: "The rod was made by one of the better companies, and was equipped with one of the new, cellular finish, floating lines. The reel was one of the more popular makes. The leader was of the newest synthetic by the largest manufacturer in this field." Or, in describing a plug, the fishing editor will say, "it was one of those banana shaped plugs that fairly shake the rod tip with their action." Why he doesn't say "it was a Flatfish" and be done with it I'll never know.

The publisher permitting, you'll find no such evasions here. In most cases, the subject will not come up; but where I believe a product, because of quality, performance, and relative cost, has an advantage over others in the field, there will be no hesitancy in naming it.

Offhand the only item of tackle that I know of offering such obvious advantages is Pfleuger's Medalist reels. For reliability, take-apart ease, wearing qualities, and superiority of drag mechanism, I know of no other reel that offers so much for the money.

Are all my reels, therefore, Medalists? No, because before Medalists became readily available after the war, I had bought a couple of reliable and fairly expensive models, which are still good, and which I will probably use until they are worn out. Also, I still have the first reel I ever owned—an old brass skeleton model single action I use for dry fly fishing on my lightest rod.

Incidentally, the man angling for larger trout would be well advised to stick to the reliable old single action. I've seen several automatics fly apart or freeze when subjected to the rampages of good-sized rainbows in fast water. Even the best and most expensive models have a habit of fouling at critical times.

As far as rods, I would attempt to advise no man in this respect. It is such a personal matter that, especially in the case of persons with considerable angling experience, little advice can be offered. Rods are much like wives, in that what suits one man might not be at all suitable for another.

I am against the idea of the all-purpose rod. Of those I have seen and used, most were frequently more costly than two specialized rods, and did not do either job as well.

Basically, the rod should fit the type of stream being fished, as well as fitting the angler. There is little to be gained and much to be lost in trying to fit the rod to the fish, or to the method.

A good example of the mistake of matching the rod to the fish comes to mind. Joe Johnson, my wife, and I walked the four miles (then) into Grebe Lake to fish for grayling one day. Because the fish ran small, seldom larger than 13 inches, I foolishly took my 7½-foot, 3½-ounce rod. And I did not think to take a spare.

When we reached the lake, a very definite hatch was on, and the fish were slashing the water to a froth. But the nearest rises were 70 feet farther than we could wade, and a very strong wind blew dead into our faces.

In trying to reach the rising fish, I overpowered the little rod, and snapped it off just above the grip. Here was a pretty kettle of no fish, four miles from the car, fish rising like mad, and no rod.

Fortunately, Joe had brought an extra, and we had good fishing until it was time to leave, and you can be sure I learned two lessons from this affair. If I'm going any distance from the car to fish, I tote an extra rod, and I match the rod to the stream or conditions under which I'll be casting, and not to the fish I expect to catch.

I replace the snake guides on my rods with light weight, non fouling spinning guides, for ease in feeding and shooting the line. If you've never tried a rod so equipped, you've got a pleasant surprise in store for you when you do.

For the wet fly fisherman, once the question of the fly has been "disputed," the next problem that arises is the line. Should it float or sink?

There are effects favorable to both types of line. The biggest adverse effect on the floating line is that the upper currents, being swifter than those at the fly level, can cause a bad drag, which not only spoils the naturalness of the drift, but raises the level of the fly.

On the other hand, the sunken line must be hauled to the surface at the end of the drift before it can be recast. This is inconvenient but not serious; it has no effect on the actual fishing of the fly. Ease and comfort in casting are nice luxuries, but they are ones with which I do not unduly concern myself. If it can be attained without sacrificing the proper fishing of the fly, fine. If it can't to heck with it. I am a fisher, not a caster. Therefore, in deeper and faster flows, I always use the sunken line. Sometimes I use my dry fly line for drifting a light fly or nymph over areas of sparse or lazy flow, but unless the fishing is very tough. I usually leave my sinking wet fly line on and use that. Mostly, I use the method that gets the fly the deepest and lets it drift most naturally. And, incidentally, don't depend on a long leader to take the place of a sunken line. It won't.

Leaders, whether wet or dry, synthetic or gut, level or tapered, should sink. Incidentally it is bad business to buy up a stock of the synthetics for future use. I once bought up a three-year supply of a tapered leader that had a rather large butt and fast taper—something rather hard to find. The company's claims not withstanding, at the start of the third year, these tested only about one-third or less of the strength that they had when new.

I lost several good fish before I got wise to what was happening. Then, I tested all of this old stock, and either cut them back to the desired strength or discarded them. At 90 cents a leader, this was a painful process. I only buy one season's stock at a time, now.

As far as hooks are concerned, this question has been debated more than any other. In her wonderful book *Favorite Flies and Their Histories,* Mary Orvis Marbury collected scores of letters from anglers all over the nation, all of whom seemed vitally interested in the hook question. This book was published in 1892, and there has been no simmering down of the matter yet.

I have tied some sixty or seventy thousand flies in the past 38 years. I've used hooks made in America, Belgium, England, Japan, Norway, and Scotland. My feeling is that American-made hooks simply are not of good enough quality to warrant using them for tying trout flies.

To be perfectly honest, I haven't used American-made hooks

in the last ten years, having found a supply of completely satis-factory hooks of British make.

Japanese hooks are in the same class as American hooks. Belgian hooks are good but almost unobtainable. Hooks made in Norway are good, reliable, and available, but the steel simply does not suit me.

Some fly tiers of note do use Norwegian hooks, but by far the largest number of top fly tiers use Scotch and English hooks. Most of the fly tiers I've talked to feel just as I do—that time and materials are far more costly than the best hooks, so it is penny wise and pound foolish not to use the very best hooks. Especially since in the end the hook is all that keeps the angler attached to his fish.

Also, the majority of fly tiers prefer plain, round bend, straight draft hooks. These are known variously as Model Perfect, Modele Parfait, Gaelic Supreme, etc. No fly tier of my acquaintance, amateur or professional, uses hooks with offset or in-curved points.

Please note we are talking about hooks for tying flies, not hooks in general. In the bait hook field, American hooks are perfectly satisfactory, and cheap in the bargain.

To put it simply, if the hook doesn't do its job, all else is nonsense.

Time was when there could be very little discussion of waders. For the serious angler, there were stocking foot or boot foot waders, and felt versus hobnailed soles. Nowadays, there are more kinds of waders than there are bees at a flower show. Most of them are pretty good.

You can get chest-type waders of light plastic, heavy plastic, rubber, rubber-coated fabric and fabric-coated rubber. Boot foot or stocking foot is still a problem, but much of the pain has been taken out of this one by new and much cheaper shoe designs for stocking-foot waders.

I'm a boot-foot man myself, but I am a lethargic type. For those pool-flitting, rock-hopping, ever-moving fellows, the stocking foot might be the wiser choice. They look a little handsomer, too, so if you're accustomed to having your picture taken while wearing a sly grin and exhibiting a couple of five pounders, maybe you should go in for the fancier footgear.

I've never needed anything but felt soles in fishing Western streams. Slime or mud covered boulders that require hobs have been pretty scarce in the streams I've fished, and this is true throughout most of the Rocky Mountain West, and Northwest. The estuary areas of some West Coast steelhead streams do get silt and slime over the rock bottoms, but, as I've said, steelhead angling is a specialized branch of trout fishing, which is outside the scope of this book.

Personally, I prefer the lightweight fabric-covered waders, but there isn't a great deal of reason behind this. They're a little more snagproof than the rubber or plastic, and do not deteriorate with age. But they're harder to patch when snagged, and cost a little more; so I suppose it comes out about even. I replace my own felt soles, since I am not at all happy with commercial felt soles. For durability and pure non-skid traction, the heavily ribbed felt soles formerly put out by Hodgman on their waders were tops, but later issues of Hodgman waders have the standard, thin, smooth felt which other less expensive waders favor.

For those that would like to do likewise, I get three-eighths-inch felt from sheet metal shops. (They use it for non-scratch paddings on work benches.) I cut out two soles and heels for each foot from this, then take them to a shoe shop and have the shoemaker sew each set together, into one pair. I have him use heavy cord, and rib stitching running across the sole every inch. This makes the most durable nonskid sole I've been able to find. Such a pair of soles will last about three seasons, and I put about 200 miles a season on my waders. I find liquid latex in tubes works fine for fastening sole to wader.

The new indoor-outdoor carpeting recently put on the market makes first-class skidproof soles. It can be obtained in one-foot squares, which will make two soles.

Waders are one of the few items in an angler's equipment that have a direct bearing on safety. I feel strongly that a man wading in heavy current over slippery rocks should have the most non-slip soles available. This is why I have stressed this subject.

There was a time I didn't use a net, which I considered a nuisance. However, I came to believe that a fish could be landed in a net with less chance of injury and a better chance of surviving if released, so I now carry one.

Any net large enough to do the job should be satisfactory. I've never found a need for the long-handled kind, but this is a matter of personal preference. I favor a very short handle, a very wide net, and quite deep. I don't want any four-pounders hanging out of my net. Those floating nets of aluminum alloy tubing are quite satisfactory. One thing: when you get them, it's a good idea to lace the net to the frame with 60-pound test nylon monofilament. I commenced doing this after having a couple of nets come loose at the rim and drop fish back into the river.

I guess I've wrestled with the problem of carrying a net as much as any other piece of gear connected with angling. If you have it hung where it is easy to reach, it's in the way. If you hang it where it doesn't entangle your legs, or some other part of your equipment, it's awkward to get at. Especially, with one hand occupied with a three-pound fish.

Lately, I've hung the net by a French snap from a ring and tape sewn to the back of the collar of my jacket or vest. It's a little unhandy to unsnap with one hand, but it is conveniently out of the way.

Herter's and Orvis both offer a net retriever, which is two feet of chain that pulls back out of sight in a case. With one of these, you can hang it on the back of your collar, net and all. When you wish to use it, flip it over your shoulder and bend over; the chain and net will extend to arm's length for easy netting. When finished with it, the spring pulls the chain back, and a flip puts the net out of the way in back. This is the most convenient way to carry a net, although some anglers may be annoyed by the retriever's thumping them in the back occasionally.

Fly books and boxes can be had in almost any size, shape, and description. Manufacturers of dry fly boxes, however, seem not to have heard that dry flies are getting larger. It is almost impossible to find a box that will hold size six and larger, and wide-hackled spiders and variants, without crushing them.

I've resorted to several devices to get boxes to hold large flies without crushing them. The most satisfactory is a lot of trouble, but worth it. I simply get two of the largest, one-inch-deep plastic boxes I can find, cut the bottoms out, and glue them together. This box will hold all the largest size dry flies that anyone would want to carry and keep them uncrushed. It is opened from either side, which is convenient. But it sure does bulge the fishing jacket.

The best wet fly container I know of is the Common Sense loose leaf book with plastic and fabric envelopes. This is a big, sturdy leather affair, which comes with six loose leaf envelopes and a leader pouch in the back. I've added an additional six envelopes to mine and each one carries from two dozen to ten dozen flies.

By proper arrangement of the envelopes, and because the contents are visible, one can find any fly of this large collection in a few seconds. There's little chance of spillage, wind has no effect, the flies are easily extracted, and it is a handsome piece of equipment if you care for that. I care for it, for this one book, a present from relatives, is my favorite piece of fishing gear.

If it seems that I'm injecting considerable personal opinion here, I plead guilty. However, I've spent many years and many dollars on tackle and gear, and it's possible some of the ideas and items mentioned here might save someone else time and money. And, incidentally, when I run into another angler who has an item of tackle or gear that fills the bill better than a similar item I am using, I do not hesitate to ask him where he got it, and to adopt it for my needs.

When it comes to creels, I have a one-track mind. The object of a creel is to keep fish fresh while carrying them. Nothing begins to approach a desert water bag for this purpose. I've used two- and three-gallon desert water bags for this purpose for over 20 years.

Some of these bags look like they were designed with this in mind. These particular bags are shallow but wide, and have a metal clip that holds the top together. This metal clip, which resembles a tube slit lengthwise, can be slipped off in a jiffy, and there's your creel. These bags also have "D" rings at the corners for snapping onto a carrying harness.

Any of these bags can easily be made into a creel by slitting the threads at the top and opening it full length. The two-gallon size will handle fish up to 15 inches. For larger fish, you'll need the three-gallon size.

These creels will keep fish a long time. Once, during 90-degree weather, I kept fish for three days in one of these bags, and they were still fresh and firm at the end of the third day. The sole precaution I took was to remove the entrails and gills and to dampen the creel well every hour or so during the day.

Washing these bags in lukewarm soda water removes any fishy

odor, and actually improves their fish-keeping qualities. Such a creel will last three seasons, provided your fishing buddy doesn't talk you out of it. This has happened to me twice.

What about fishing jackets and vests? Well, I own some, and I will probably own some more. The commercial models all have minor faults, so I've taken to making my own. (With my wife's help.)

In a jacket, I want roomy sleeves first. I do a lot of fishing in sleet, rain, snow, and cold, so I want to be able to wear thermal underwear, a wool shirt and a sweater under my fishing jacket and still have arm room. After roomy sleeves, my next thought is for big, roomy pockets and lots of them. My big dry fly box and my wet fly book require big bellows-type pockets. It is true that when I put these in my vest and put it on, I look like I'm wearing water wings. Well, so be it. I cannot be parted with either article, so glamor must go.

The lack of bellows-type pockets is the major fault I find in most jackets and vests. An ordinary flat pocket which measures 5 x 9 inches is strained to bursting by a fly box 8 x 4 x 1 inch deep.

The best-made vests and jackets, run considerably higher in price than those of somewhat lesser quality. I have seen jackets costing $45 and vests costing $27 that were actually only of slightly better quality than those costing half as much. I would put $17 for a jacket and $12 for a vest as the top price one should pay and still expect to get value received (as of 1968.)

I insist on all jackets and vests having a big pocket across the back. This should be at least 12 inches deep, and zippered across both ends. A loop of old fly line nine or ten inches long fastened to the zipper foot will allow easier opening and closing of this pocket while wearing the garment. It isn't necessary or even desirable for this pocket to be lined with rubber or plastic. No matter what it's lined with, it's the poorest creel in creation. But it's fine for toting lunch, a towel for wiping the hands, the rain jacket, extra reels, a copy of *The Compleat Angler,* or a flask of old Razor Blades.

The rain jacket is a must, at least for older anglers. When I was 20 or so, I didn't mind fishing for hours in a pouring rain, sleet, or driving snow, with no rain gear. But, to paraphrase Corey

Ford, rain is getting wetter, sleet colder, and snow thicker these days. I still fish many days a year in rain, sleet, and snow, and thanks to a good rain jacket, I still enjoy it.

Fortunately, there are any number of fine rain jackets on the market. All of them will do the job of protecting the wearer; many of them will fold into a package the size of a hearty sandwich.

The better jackets of plastic are those that remain limp and pliable at or below 20 degrees F. A hood is a very desirable feature.

Along with the rain jacket, hood, and waders, medical rubber gloves are nice. They keep the hands dry, afford excellent line and rod control, and contribute a little warmth. They are well worth the expense, and they also protect the hands from mosquitoes.

Any well-fitting, cuffless pair of trousers will serve as under-wader pants. Whether they are cotton or wool depends mostly on the temperature of the water being waded. But they must be cuffless for comfort.

One inconvenience that manifests itself while you don waders over pants is the tendency for the pants to climb and bunch up. Cure this by sewing a loop of half-inch elastic to each side of each pant leg at the bottom. The length is correct when the elastic puts just a bit of tension under the arch of the foot when you stand erect.

Cushion soled hiking socks of heavy wool are hard to beat for boot foot waders. A pair of lighter nylon socks may be worn beneath them if chafing is a problem.

Chafing is a problem with stocking foot waders. I know of only one way to solve it. This is to cement a flap of material to the wader leg just above where the shoe top comes. This flap should go completely around the leg and should be about six inches long. A lace should be fitted to the bottom of the flap, either by eyelets or by turning the flap back upon itself to form a tube to encase the lace.

After the shoes and socks are donned these flaps are pulled down over the top of the shoe and pulled tight by the flap laces. This prevents sand and gravel from working down inside the shoe and chafing the waders—and the feet. It only takes a few minutes to put these on a pair of waders, and they will double their life.

There are any number of perfectly adequate fly line dressings on the market, but if there is a single suitable dry fly oil, I've never seen it, nor do I know anyone who has. Silicones waterproof to beat the band—until a husky trout has mangled the fly and soaked it in blood and slime. Then, after washing the fly clean, it resembles a sponge. Dry the fly and soak it in more silicone? Sure, if you've got an hour to wait until the silicone dries. Other oils are greasy and mat the hackles, some leave an oily ring on the water, others contain ingredients that harm the line or rod finish.

The only satisfactory dry fly preparation of which I know is a simple solution of lighter fluid and paraffin. The exact proportion of the two ingredients can be left to the individual. For me, a teaspoon of melted paraffin to two ounces of lighter fluid is fine.

This preparation acts as an efficient cleaner, evaporates promptly, is not harmful to finishes, and the congealed wax stiffens the hackle. If the mixture leaves a readily discernible whitish film on the hackle, it needs a dash more lighter fluid.

For drying a mangled fly, after a trout has chomped on it, facial tissues in a thick pad are ideal. I prefer the darker pastel tissues so that I don't have to turn my back on the stream every-time I dry the fly.

The answer to sinking leaders is not to be found in bottle or tube. Instead, synthetics with a specific gravity heavier than one is the solution. I do find that even with the heaviest it is now and then necessary to rub a little mud or slime on the dry fly leader, which has a tendency to get a film of dry fly solution on that portion near the fly which is the crucial area—the portion you most want to sink.

I find that rubbing synthetics with a fold of chamois does a better job of removing kinks than anything else. By keeping the chamois wet, it also aids the sinking process.

I seldom employ weight on the leader, choosing instead to put it under the body of the fly. If extremely high water or strong current calls for more weight, I wind lead fuse wire on the leader —the same type used for weighting the fly. It is cheaper, easier to use, and more convenient to carry than shot, and any amount from a grain to an ounce can be put on as required. It can be used over and over until lost, and saves wear and tear on the teeth.

[14]

Solving the Problem

When the angler arrives at his chosen stream—rod in hand, hope in heart—he is immediately faced with The Problem: What fly and what presentation should be used to start the day's fishing?

I have known some relatively advanced anglers who say no such problem exists, except in the mind of the angler. I have fished with these gentlemen, and watched with amusement as they arrive at the stream's edge, step into the water, and immediately start flailing away. They don't give a single thought to what the fish might be taking, they say. It's the method and the angler's skill that count. They intend to find the method by going through their routines until some fish obliges them, I guess.

This does not seem to me to be a very intelligent approach to a sport that has occupied and fascinated some of the greatest minds in history. It would seem to me that this hit-or-miss approach, which apparently is widely used, is one of the reasons anglers greet each other with, "What luck?"

It is not possible to step up to the stream, look at the water, squint at the sky, test the wind, and then tie on the exact fly and use the exact presentation called for. But it is possible—using past experience, knowledge of the stream, its insect life, the temperature, the weather, and a little logic—to arrive at a selection of fly and method that will be something more than a haphazard guess.

Oddly enough, there are anglers who carry the scientific method of selecting the fly and the method to the opposite extreme. It takes all kinds of people to make a world, and an angler's world is diverse as anyone's.

There used to be an angler who, I'm told, fished every summer in Yosemite Valley and Tuolumne Meadows. He was called "The Professor" and with good reason. He was tall and stooped, with an absent minded expression that was a true reflection of his mental state, and he was ultra scientific in his approach to selecting the fly and the method.

I was fortunate enough to see "The Professor" in action at close range a couple of times. I was pretty young, and new at trout fishing, and was impressed. His demonstration of the scientific technique would have impressed far wiser anglers than I.

Approaching the stream, he would unstrap a nicely finished, brass-bound box from his shoulder, open it up, take a large ledger from its cover, and lay it aside. Then he would commence his tests. He would set up a small thermometer in the shade of his box, on the lid of which was an aneroid barometer. Another thermometer with a small sinker and piece of line attached, he lowered into the stream.

For testing the clarity of the stream, he used a porcelain device on which was painted, in quarter-inch squares, the colors of the spectrum. Mounting this on the end of a jointed pole, he thrust it down into a deep section of the stream until only one color

A fine, fast run; every area can be probed with a fly. Angling pressure will drive trout from this hold by midsummer.

remained visible. Then he would withdraw it slowly, noting at which depth each subsequent color became visible. (The rod was marked every six inches.)

All the data from these experiments were noted into the ledger, plus the weather condition (he used five terms to express conditions from completely clear to completely overcast.)

After all this was entered he would go through the ledger, checking here and there, h'm'ming to himself, very much the picture of the scientific researcher. Presently, he would find what he was looking for and put away the ledger. Out would come a diary, which was opened to a certain page and read intently. Then, and only then, were the instruments returned to their case, the case returned to the car, and the gentleman went fishing.

I was in those days what you might call nosey. I hadn't yet learned the tact and diplomacy that would allow my prying to be called curiosity. However, the old gentleman not only wasn't angry at my blunt questions, he was pleased that I asked them.

Sitting me down on a rock, he lit his pipe, waved out the match, and regaled me as follows:

"My dear boy," he said, "no need to apologize at all. There is far too little honest, unashamed curiosity among young people these days. Besides, as Walton says, 'are we not brothers of the angle and sharers of all good secrets?'

"There are many, many reasons why men fish. Most of them, and fly fishers most of all, do not really fish to fill the creel. I have heard it said, and possibly you also, that fishermen go to catch fish, and anglers go fishing. I do not know if the distinction is worthwhile, but in any event, few men would enjoy angling if catching fish were all there were to it.

"Each man cherishes one or more of the multitude of joys of angling. Those he cherishes most, he spends the most time pursuing. But, the more educated or intelligent a man becomes, the more he must have a reason for enjoying himself.

"In my case, I try to reduce the amount that luck, or pure chance, plays in catching fish. The more I do so, the more skill enters into the picture, the more the sport becomes an art and a science.

"Also," he said dryly, "It proves how much more intelligent I am than the fish."

He then went on to tell me how his system worked. Briefly, he noted the water temperature, the air temperature, the barometric pressure corrected to sea level, the cloud cover or lack of it, and the extreme water visibility. After setting these items down, in a specific order, in his ledger, he then went back through the ledger to previous days that showed approximately the same figures. Then he would turn in the diary to those particular dates, where he would read what insect activity had taken place, what kind, the time, the size of any fish caught, and what had been the taking fly and method.

I was not surprised when he told me that his ledger contained notes concerning all the streams in the area.

He fished about one hundred days a year, he said, and his ledger would hold ten years' notes on a dozen streams. He had other ledgers for other areas. There were, of course, several diaries with daily results, for each ledger.

Few men would care to be so scientific, but I have adopted The Professor's methods, and have added to it tests for water hardness and oxygen content. I do not use it daily, but at least once weekly during the season I test and fish three streams (the same three all the time) and in a few years hope to show that there is a pattern, and that a few, uncomplicated observations will enable one to pick the right fly and presentation most of the time, based on this voluminous background research.

For now, for regular fishing when I arrive at a stream, I make a guess at the water and air temperatures, water clarity, and try to remember what insect activity I detected on this stream last time the conditions were similar.

If there is evidence of fish feeding, of course, the above is superfluous. In this case, I find a vantage point, whip out the binoculars and devote a few minutes to study. Usually, I can get the right fly and method the first time.

If no feeding activity is in evidence, then I am back to trying to recall what went on last time under these conditions. Then I try the same flies and methods, modified as experience tells me.

If I am unable to recall the flies and methods, or can remember no similar set of conditions, I have to try something else.

Is it stone fly or mayfly water? Is the water temperature such that nymphs will be active? Are there any dragon fly nymphs in this stretch? What about caddis? Helgramites?

With no insect activity or signs of fish feeding in evidence, my rules are fairly simple. I select the largest type insect found in the stretch, and choose an imitation of that for my tail fly. For the dropper, I choose an imitation of another prevalent insect, of as different a type as possible. If the water is over two feet deep, and the current strong, both flies will be weighted. If the current is not too swift, only the tail fly will be weighted.

In fishing the sunken fly, the first choice of method is invariably the deep natural drift. If, after thoroughly covering the first stretch of holding water, there are no strikes, a change is indicated.

Let us say that the first area fished was a fast, medium-deep, boulder-lined run. In the West, this is most apt to be stone fly water. There may be mayfly nymphs present too, but if so, they are usually small. No matter—a stone fly nymph will pass for both. For the dropper fly, then, we should use a caddis, cased or uncased, or a general type fly such as the wooly worm.

Only after the original brace of flies have been given a fair test through several methods of presentation should they be changed. The next choice is not so simple and often results in a guess-and-grab attack on the fly-book. My second choice is usually a drastic change. If my first flies were large and dark, then my second brace will be smaller and brighter. I usually do *not* move on to another location. If there are trout in the stretch I am fishing they are as good as any to work on until the taking fly and method is found.

I base the above on the evidence that a carefully fished wet fly or nymph does not frighten or otherwise disturb the fish. My underwater explorations have verified this time and again. Therefore, why wear out your wader soles and yourself? Rest the stretch a spell while you put on your thinking cap.

As you have seen, I prefer the leisurely approach, with more thinking and less thrashing. When I first became a trout fisherman, I would race madly to the water's edge, plunge in, and start casting like beating rugs. I thought that the more casts I got in, the better chance I had. You see, I then thought that catching fish was a matter of luck. It isn't.

One of my favorite stretches of stream—perhaps my very favorite—is that section of the Madison River in Yellowstone Park from the cable car crossing downstream to a mile above Baker's

Hole. It is just ten miles from my home, and is one of the major reasons I live where I do.

This stretch comprises several miles of stream. There are scores of good holding areas, and hundreds of small spot-lies, in it. At the beginning of the stretch is a fast, deep run known locally as Hole Number One. This run is something of a puzzler; at times it will provide the finest kind of fishing, while at other times no amount of skill and effort will produce a worthwhile fish, even when the rest of the stream is turning out good catches. From experience, and from talking to other anglers, I know this condition exists elsewhere. For years, I wondered about it, and believe I have found the reason.

I must admit that I have no hard and fast figures on which to base my solution. Observation has shown, however, that this hold, being the first fishworthy stretch for some distance, and also the first convenient spot to approach the stream for over a mile, received intense angling pressure. While it was an excellent hold in many respects, there was no area of it that could not be probed with the fly.

My guess it that the fish, having no place to hide, were eventually driven out of the area by the herd of anglers. Of course, some of the fish were caught out, but it has been my experience that when fish are caught and removed from good lies, other fish immediately move into these lies. Nearly always there are more fish in a stream than the number of good lies.

My theory, then, is that fish were not moving into this area to replace fish caught out, because of constant pounding during the day. This is somewhat borne out by the fact the best chance to take fish from this hold was during the early morning. between daylight and sunrise. Even then, after the season was well under way, rarely was a good fish taken.

Once I recognized that my chances were poor in this stretch during the main portion of the season, I quit spending the two hours necessary to thoroughly cover the hold, and started fishing somewhere else. Late in the season, after Labor Day, this hold would begin to produce some very good fish.

The point here is that, while it is well and good to spend sufficient time to fish a hold thoroughly, it also must be realized that it is possible to spend too much time on unproductive areas. There is no guide to this problem, it is simply a matter of knowing local conditions well enough.

It sometimes happens that an area isn't barren, but is occupied by a big, bully fish who will have none of your ordinary persuasions, and will not allow other fish into his area. Usually, this involves a rather small but excellent holding area, since such a fish cannot protect more than a few square yards.

Ignoring the rare exceptions above, it pays one, on starting the day, to cover the water well, with the best possible choice of fly and method.

Nobody knows, I suppose, what preverseness causes fish to ignore a carefully presented fly at nine o'clock and to smash the same fly presented in the same manner at three o'clock. It does happen, and on the occasions when it does, it often appears that no fly or manner of presentation will produce results until the fish are ready. Then, sometime later in the day, the fish will willingly take the same fly presented in the same manner that brought no results earlier.

At times like these, the two-man-team technique is appropriate, if one has a companion. One angler should continue to use the same cast of flies, with varying forms of presentation, while the other angler should change flies every 30 minutes or so. This provides the best opportunity to solve the problem, with the least wasted effort.

Why not have both anglers change flies? Well, over the years, experience has shown that, under the conditions cited, the changing of flies accomplishes very little. Therefore, the only reason for doing it is because no specific way has been found yet to absolutely identify this condition. Thus, if you have a companion, one of you should change flies on the chance that the fish actually do want a different bill of fare.

Once I was fishing the Madison with Joe Johnson when we found the fish unwilling. We stayed with it, fishing steadily through the day. I did not change my cast of Montana Stone Fly nymph and brown wooly worm, nor did I move from the fine stretch of holding water where we started fishing. Joe changed flies immediately and moved on downstream.

About 3:30 in the afternoon the fish began to hit and I had excellent fishing until dark. About an hour after dark, Joe returned to the car, and we compared notes.

I had stayed put and never changed flies. Joe had fished a total of more than three miles of stream and changed flies a dozen times. He had not had a strike until about 3:30, then he too had had excellent fishing. So, in this case, the answer to the problem was just to continue fishing until the fish were ready.

The above has happened to me many times—so often, in fact, that I have developed a decided reluctance to change flies just because action isn't immediately forthcoming. This calls for intelligent selection of the first flies used, and demands of you the confidence that you have made the right choice.

On days when like conditions have existed, and I had no fishing companion, I have attempted to query other anglers after the close of the day's fishing. Invariably, they started taking fish about the same time of day that I did, although most likely on different flies.

This would indicate, say those the-method-is-all-that-counts boys that they have been proven correct. Hardly. While it's true that other anglers were taking fish on different flies, it is not true that their catches were identical. The larger number of anglers I have queried about this matter have had just a few fish, mostly small. Usually, their choice of flies, or at least the flies on which they had taken fish, were small, lightly tied flies, and in many cases, were non-imitative of any insect group. Those who had made good catches of lusty fish had selected flies representative of the actual insects in the stream, and usually, though not always, their flies ran larger.

So, there will be days when the only way to solve the problem is to wait the fish out. There will also be days when the fish appear inactive, and waiting them out will not help. How to tell one situation from the other is the problem.

On any given day when I achieve no results within the first hour, I know that I have one of the above situations. To solve it, should I persist with my original choice of flies or try something else?

At this point, if alone, I stop fishing and with binoculars and naked eye, begin to look for insect or fish activity. I examine known stretches of feeding water for the telltale flash of a feeding fish. I scan the air and the water for the appearance of a fly or two.

If I get no answers here, it's time to take other steps. Trying to find a place where I can look directly into a fish's lie is one method. The purpose here is to find a fish that can be observed without alarming it. Once found, I spend at least 15 minutes in close observation before I come to a decision.

If the fish is lying almost completely motionless, moving tail and fin just enough to hold position, then he is a non-feeding fish. If he sways a little from side to side, or varies his level, he is interested and will feed if something suitable comes along right in his feeding groove.

If the fish is constantly swinging here and there—moving up, dropping back, changing his level—he is looking for food and will examine almost anything that comes within his range of vision. If he is rooting among the rocks, he is, of course, actively feeding, but feeding deep.

If the case is number one, the non-feeding fish, you will have to wait him out. Changing flies will do little good, and changing methods probably will not work either. However, since there is no way of knowing just when the fish will start to feed, you must continue your efforts.

In case number two, precision casting to a known lie is the answer. Such a fish probably would not move over a foot either way, no matter how tempting the tidbit.

A fish ranging widely from his lie but constantly returning to a given spot is wanting to feed, and will seize just about any natural appearing lure that comes along. This is the most common state of fish, and regular methods of fishing the wet fly or nymph will probably be successful.

Our deep feeding fish calls for a nymph-type fly drifted deeply and naturally, using many casts and drifts. Cover the hold thoroughly and deeply and you should get action.

While we speak of a single fish, of course, that is not literally what is meant. I am sure that all of us know that the behavior pattern of fish is such that, in most cases, the actions of one are indicative of the actions of many.

The cases just covered all concern fish that are either deep, inactive, or both. If the fish are in shallow water, or are actively feeding near or on the surface, it will be evident, and your method accordingly indicated.

Perhaps you wonder why we don't spend an hour or so on observation before we commence to fish. The answer is, that fish are seldom in a complete non-feeding state where waiting them out is the answer. So, over the years, you will save time by trying them first, then switching to study if no action is forthcoming.

It may seem odd, but a great many anglers are reluctant to spend any time in observation. The reason for this is unknown to me. On the whole, I would guess I have spent about one third as many hours observing fish as I have fishing for them. In my youth, I spent many hours up in trees leaning over the water, watching the fish. At the time, I wasn't "studying" them, but was just watching because I was curious, and entertained. Later, when I went to reexamine it, this stored-up knowledge was very helpful in furthering my understanding of trout.

I still spend much time in observation. Sometimes I sit on the bank near a long straight stretch and use the binoculars. Other times, I lie on my belly on the bank and look down into a medium deep run. For specific answers, during research on a particular problem, I don face mask and breathing apparatus and get down on the stream bottom. This latter is going a little far for the average angler, but the other activities will be worthwhile.

It does little good to observe the fish if study of fish environment is left out. The factors of weather, water type, temperature, clarity, and insect activity must be correlated with fish activity if one is to analyze the actions of the fish.

The ultimate purpose, of course, is to determine the fly and the method that will interest the fish. And remember—we are not only interested in the present, but in the future. Study, analysis, and practice when added together total knowledge. If any one factor is missing, there will be a gap in knowledge that will render it nearly useless for solving the problem of what fly and what method.

It should be quite apparent that water clarity and condition are important factors to be considered in selecting the fly and method. Clarity affects both choices, so let's consider it first.

Range of vision, the distance at which the fly can be detected, is dependent upon the color of the fly and the clarity of the water. The fly's size enters into this also, since it is obvious that a larger fly can be detected at a greater distance than could a smaller fly of the same pattern. Since the fish must detect the fly by eyesight alone, we must have a good idea of how close we must drift the fly to the fish's lie before it will be detected. In most clear streams, this is not a serious problem. In amber, muddy, or other discolored streams, it distinctly is.

One way to tell at what distance the fly can be seen in any particular stream is to lower the fly into the water, and judge at what depth it becomes indistinct. Note I said "indistinct," not "invisible." A feeding fish might move to investigate an object indistinctly seen, but we are mostly concerned here with fish that are not actively feeding. In any case, you must be sure the fish has an adequate opportunity to see your fly.

Some colors of the spectrum are visible at greater distances than others, in air. In water, these same colors might not be readily visible. In amber or tea colored water, a reddish brown fly, such as the Brown Hackle, will be invisible at even a very short distance. If the water is discolored somewhat with mud, a ginger-colored fly will disappear from view within a foot or so. So, water clarity or color must be considered in choosing the fly. It was this that the Professor, mentioned earlier in this chapter, was testing with his jointed pole and enameled porcelain.

If the water is moving swiftly and there are numerous obstacles to the current, bubbles, cross currents, and light refraction will cut down on visibility. Also, the fish has a shorter look at the fly, due to the current speed. Therefore, a fly used in such areas should be bulkier than one used in a smooth topped gliding run.

In pockets among rapids, or other very fast stretches, the fish generally sees the fly in silhouette or as a fleeting shadow. There is little time to examine it—it is now or never. A fly for these areas should be large, and rely heavily on shape as well as color.

In areas of very clear water, with slow moving current, the fly can be much smaller; in fact it should be. The fish has excellent visibility here, and time to examine your offering thoroughly. A large fly will be detected as a fraud in most cases. This kind of fishing calls for sparsely-tied, slender-bodied flies of non-contrasting colors. Unless there are weed beds present, your fish from this type water are apt to run small.

Oxygen content of the water has a decided effect on fish activity. In summer, streams of fluctuating level generally lose oxygen as the day progresses, with a consequent reduction in fish activity. Such streams are best fished in early morning, or very late afternoon and evening, during the summer months.

Constant level streams usually do not fluctuate seriously in oxygen content. They tend generally, though not always, to run cooler than fluctuating streams. On such streams, which are cool, fish activity during the summer months increases toward midday. The contrast between these two type streams results in the apparent paradox wherein one angler relates he took all his fish in the early morning while another vows the middle of the day is the taking period.

In most areas, most streams are of the fluctuating type. In some parts of the country, there are no other kind. Anglers from such sections are so accustomed to very early morning fishing that it becomes an ingrained habit. It is such habits that must be guarded against in solving the fishing problem.

One October, an angler from the East was staying in the same cabin camp in West Yellowstone as I and my family. We became friendly, and arranged to go fishing together one day. Although the weather was on the cool side, the air temperature got up to 70 or so degrees during the middle of the day. It fell to about 15 degrees every night.

Nevertheless, my new friend insisted upon arising at four o'clock the next morning; we were on the stream well before six. It was icy cold, with deep frost everywhere, and puddles frozen in the shallows.

We had not a strike until nearly noon, but from then until about three o'clock, we had excellent fishing. My new friend thought it quite strange to be taking fish during the "heat" of the day. I pointed out to him that in a stream well supplied with oxygen as was the one we were fishing, fish activity was dependent on the water's warming. In streams of less oxygen content, activity would cease at higher temperatures. I don't believe I ever convinced him, because he continued to be on the stream before sunrise all the time he stayed in West Yellowstone.

So, part of solving the problem lies in not overlooking certain basic factors. These—the ones we have just covered concerning water clarity, condition, temperature, and oxygen content—bear heavily on fish activity and have much to do with selection of fly and method. If any one of them is ignored, we are back to the chuck-and-chance-it school of fishing.

Suppose we've considered all the factors, made our most informed choice of fly and method, and cover the water well, but still get no results. Further, suppose observation has indicated that some feeding activity is taking place, and our method is suited to this activity. Still we get no strikes. What can be wrong?

This condition exists more often than one would think, and in my opinion the solving of it separates the men from the boys. Only advanced anglers will solve these situations with any regularity.

One such condition has been discussed in another chapter. This is the "nuisance" rise. There are several variations of this one, most of which involve the fish actually feeding on something other than what they appear to be.

For instance, I've seen several cases where a nice hatch of Hendrickson (Ephemerella invaria) was on, and the fish were rising nicely. The Hendrickson or Blue Quill number 12 matched the hatch well but took no fish, no matter how beautifully the fly was presented. The reason? The fish were actually feeding on hatching caddis of about size 18, and doing such a thorough job that almost none of the caddis escaped to be seen by the angler. The Firehole and upper Madison still have hatches like this every year, and I see many frustrated anglers beating the water during these periods. Solving this one is just a case of looking very closely at what is going on. Frankly, I might have gone years without knowing, if it hadn't been for my using binoculars in such situations.

So, if you're apparently doing everything right, fish are feeding, but you aren't catching any, take a closer, longer look at the fish. You've missed something.

Sometimes, fish appear to be grubbing for nymphs, but will have none of the best nymph presentations. This one can be a stopper. To be frank, sometimes I can solve it and sometimes I can't.

On some occasions, where the current speed will allow it, this one can be handled by creeping a weighted nymph across the bottom. This requires a slow, deliberate retrieve with many pauses. The object is to try to simulate a creeping nymph. It's a tough task.

If current speed is such that the above method is not feasible, working the nymph on the bottom near the break in the current may be possible. One fellow I know, in circumstances like these, pinches split shot on his leader every six inches until he achieves some control over his creeping nymph. Often it takes six or more shot to do the job.

Such a rig cannot be cast; it must be awkwardly swung and tossed, somewhat like throwing a lariat. Most fly fishermen, like myself, are enamored with the flow and rhythm of casting, and would rather give this cumbersome method a pass.

Early in the season, whether streams are high or normal, insect activity is reduced. The fish at this time are apt to be voracious, but not too active. Exactly why this is, I'm not sure, but it happens almost every spring.

At this time, if other methods fail, a large, bulky streamer or bucktail type fly, drifted along with only an occasional twitch, will often work. However, repeated drifts through the same area are necessary. The fish, although they seem to want a large mouthful, won't move far or fast to take it.

This same attitude occurs in late fall, just before freezeup. There is one difference at this time: the same type of fly and presentation will work, but the fish will move a short distance to take the fly. The take is usually savage—a smash that often finds me with a broken leader.

I've thought about this problem a great deal, and it seems to me that the reasons behind the fish's attitude are the same for both conditions. Cold water makes the fish inactive—stiff, one might say. In the spring, the water has been cold for a long period, and the fish are well chilled. They stir reluctantly. In the fall, the fish are just becoming chilled, and tend to move a little more readily.

In spring, the fish are hungry from their long fast. In fall, they sense the onset of winter, and their hunger is aroused. In both cases, they want a big mouthful without too much effort.

My reasoning on this may be wrong. Whatever the reason, this condition exists in early spring and late fall, and the fly and presentation described have worked best for me.

The above situation is a good example of why we must take the temperature into consideration when arriving at a choice of fly and method. We also have to consider the weather over a period of time preceding the day we are fishing. One cold day will not lower water temperature much; two weeks or more of chilly weather will. Cold rain for a couple of days will chill a stream.

So will snow.

In the spring, we are more apt to be aware of the effect of temperature. In the fall, we may forget, especially if we've had a few days of balmy weather.

A week of cold weather followed by a warm day will see the fish active late in the day if at all. One or two more warm days, however, will start them moving. Always, in solving the problem, it is well to consider the present weather, and conditions that have prevailed for the past several days as well, before arriving at a conclusion. Remember the story of the math professor who wrote the mathematical problem $\dfrac{6}{4}$ on the blackboard and asked the class: "What's the answer?"

Quickly one alert student asked, "What's the problem?"

Always try to ascertain what the problem is before attempting to solve it.

⟦15⟧

The Weather and Other Factors

Meteorologists, those curious people who study the weather and issue weather reports, have some queer ideas about weather.

For a number of years I was connected with an organization that made constant use of all kinds of weather data. One day, when most of the office force was on vacation, the boss looked up from what he was doing and said, "Call up the weather station and get the present weather, will you?"

So, I called and relayed the request. "There's no weather to-day," replied the pleasant voice at the other end of the line. For a moment, I was taken aback, then I remembered that "Weather" to a weather man means precipitation or storms. An ideal day to most of us, would mean "no weather" to a weather man.

Ever since Izaak, and maybe before, anglers have been deeply concerned with the weather, and the number of theories about the effect of weather on fishing has therefore grown with the years.

Mostly, when it comes to actually going fishing, I ignore the weather. To me, the best time to go fishing is when you can get away. To be sure, I do take note of the air temperature, before selecting the fly and method for the first attempt.

Also, I give some consideration to cloud cover, or lack of it. The amount of light has a direct bearing on the range of vision (of a fish), and on the appearance of a fly. Thus, this aspect of "weather" is of some importance.

Beyond those two factors I do not go, in planning my campaign.

However, the complete weather picture is recorded in my notes on those dates when I am "testing" a stream.

The direction of the wind has no effect at all on the fishing. I have made record catches on days when the wind was from any direction but straight up. I have made excellent catches when the wind was boxing the compass—blowing from all quarters of the globe in turn.

As a matter of fact, any wind is a help when one is dry fly fishing on quiet waters. A ruffle on the water improves one's chances from several standpoints: it allows the fisherman to go unseen while delivering his cast; it blows insects into the water, so that the fish expect food on the surface when the wind blows; and if the cast should be bungled slightly, it will probably go unnoticed when the wind is blowing.

Too much wind is a nuisance, yet I've caught many fine trout when the wind was blowing a gale. Such strong winds undoubtedly distract the fisherman, but unless they blow for days, they probably do not bother the fish.

The finest day's dry fly fishing I ever had came on a day when a strong, fitful, and gusty wind was blowing. I was fishing the Firehole in Biscuit Basin. The fish had been rising well for several days, but the air had been so still that they were exceedingly shy.

About ten in the morning on this particular day, the wind began to blow, and almost immediately I was into a good fish. In the lulls between gusts, I didn't do a thing, but a cast made while the wind was blowing was nearly always good for fish.

I left the stream about 3:30 in the afternoon. I had hooked and landed 29 trout, only one weighing less than a pound. The top fish, the only one I kept, weighed better than three pounds.

It was this day that made me realize how valuable the wind can be to the dry fly fisherman. Since then, I've tended to fish the dry fly more when the wind was blowing, and have had excellent results. Also, strong winds often make proper fishing of the wet fly difficult, so the whole thing is in the angler's favor.

Barometric pressure and its effect on the fish has been an item of great interest for the past several decades. Some angler-writers have gone to great lengths to formulate theories on the effect of a falling barometer on fishing. The consensus is that a falling barometer causes poor fishing.

My experiments in this area show that the theory tends to be

true only for certain varying level streams. And the effect is the
result of the same cause as rising water temperature. That is, a
falling barometer allows escape of dissolved oxygen from the
water, and the effect is that fish reduce their activity, if the oxygen
content drops below comfortable levels.

A constant-level (spring-fed) stream replenishes its oxygen supply more readily, and a falling barometer seems to have little or
no effect on fish activity in such streams.

In the Yellowstone area, both types of stream can be found in
relatively close proximity, so that it is quite simple to check this
particular theory. I've made scores of such checks with results as
stated.

As far as the effect of low or high barometric pressure is concerned, I maintain that the pressure level has no effect whatever
on fish activity. I base this on the fact that altitude affects pressure, and that one can, in the Yellowstone area, find trout streams
from 4500-foot elevations on up to 7500-foot elevations. That
would correspond to a pressure change roughly equal to three
inches of mercury. Or to put it differently, if the pressure was
26.92 by the barometer at 7500 feet, the reading at 4500 feet,
in the same general area, would be about 29.92.

The first figure would represent a low barometric pressure in
comparison to the second. If actual pressures have anything to do
with fish activity, one should detect a difference of activity between
the fish at the different altitudes. I have been able to detect no
such differences when moving rapidly from one elevation to the
other for the specific purpose of checking this theory.

I've checked this one often, fishing first at one elevation, then
moving to another, then back to the first. Near my home, I can
be fishing at 4500 feet one hour, and the next be fishing at 7500
feet. Repeated checks by changing locations have shown no de-
tectable difference in the fishing on a given day. As a result, I am
convinced that stable barometric pressure as such, whether high
or low, has no effect on fishing.

So, a falling barometer may adversely affect the fishing on those
streams which are critical in dissolved oxygen supply. These are
the same streams that would be adversely affected by higher water
temperatures (75-80 degrees F.) and the effect is a reduction in
overall fish activity. These streams can be identified in most cases
by high water in spring, which recedes in summer, and leaves large

areas of stream bed exposed in the late-summer months. A stream not subject to rapid or extreme fluctuations of water level is not apt to have its fishing affected by barometric pressure changes.

Air temperature for a given day has little effect on fish activity. But if high or low temperatures continue for some weeks, the stream temperature will respond in the same direction. This will affect fish activity. Very low water temperatures (40-55 degrees F.) will cause fish to reduce activity. They will also affect the fish's metabolism and he will eat less food, and less often.

Hot water pours constantly into the Firehole. Fishing remains good.

At the other end of the scale, water temperatures in the 75-80 degree range produce the best of possible fishing *if* the stream has a good oxygen supply. So, if there has been a prolonged hot spell, your best chance for good fishing is in a spring-fed creek or other constant-level stream. And it doesn't have to be cold springs that feed the stream. The Firehole is fed by a great many hot springs, and the temperature tops 80 degrees in late summer. The fishing remains great.

The same water temperatures that affect fish affect aquatic insects in largely the same way. It also appears that lack of oxygen in the water affects fish and insects alike, but I haven't enough data yet to be sure about this one. It seems a reasonable conclusion.

Cloud cover is important partly from the standpoint of its effect on the range of vision of the fish. A secondary effect is that the fly looks different in direct sunlight and in shadow. This latter effect is the more serious of the two.

Most anglers probably don't notice it, but many flies that are effective in bright sunshine become just ordinary fish catchers in the shadows. Conversely, some flies do very well in the shadows but are literally worthless in bright sun. Dry flies are more critical in this respect than are sunken flies.

It was in 1948 that I first noticed the effect of sunlight and shadow on the fish-taking capabilities of flies. I was fishing the Firehole, working my way upstream from below Biscuit Basin. Most of the area was timbered and in shadow.

My fly was a size 16 Tups Indispensable. Fishing the rises near the banks and log jams, I did nicely, taking fish in the one- to two-pound class.

The fish were rising in the same manner in the meadows. However, these fish would have none of my fly. Time and again I drifted it over rising fish, but there were no takers. Puzzled, I dropped back to the timbered stretch I had just left, and immediately took a good fish.

For awhile, I thought leader shadow was the trouble. However, drifting the fly in such a manner that it was between me and the fish brought no rises in the meadow. Reluctantly, I decided it was the fly. I changed to a size 16 Adams and the fish in the meadows gobbled it up.

Further experimenting showed the fish in the timber accepted the Tups or the Adams with equal fervor. In the sunlit meadows, the Tups was completely ignored.

Since then, the same thing has happened a number of times. The problem is less acute with the wet fly, but there have been days when fish stopped taking a certain wet fly when the sun came out from behind the clouds. On sunny days, I've had fish stop hitting when clouds covered the sun.

Sometimes the answer is to wait out the change of light. But if it's going to last a while, it may pay to change flies. Unfortunately, I cannot give any advice on what flies work best in the sun or which ones are better in the shadows. As **they** say in the musicians' union, you'll just have to play this one by ear.

I'm fond of fishing in the rain, if it isn't a downpour. Possibly this is because I've had some of my most successful days when it was raining.

There are several good reasons for fishing to be good in rainy weather. Rain cools stream temperatures if they are high, or raises them if the water is cold, in most cases. It beats considerable oxygen into the water. It washes food into the stream. Sometimes it discolors the water, which encourages wary fish to feed more boldly. And it breaks up the surface, hiding the angler from the fish.

The above factors influence some streams more than others. Streams which are too warm, too cold, or deficient in oxygen will benefit more than other streams. Since there are **many** streams in most areas filling this category, improved fishing during rainy weather is something to look for. This is especially true in late summer. Also, expect the better fishing just after rain starts.

Prolonged heavy rain seems, in most cases, to be detrimental to fishing. However, after streams start to clear, or lower after heavy rains, good fishing is the rule. Just why this should be I don't know, but it is invariably so.

Violent thunderstorms and hail seem to stop fish activity at once. I don't know the reason for this, but believe vibration has something to do with it. I do know that in 1959, following an earthquake (near West Yellowstone), the fishing was affected by the aftershocks. Many a day I would be fishing along, doing very well, when a tremor would occur. Immediately, the fish would stop hitting for an hour or more. Every tremor violent enough to be detected by the fisherman brought a sudden halt to fish activity.

Sleet or snow early in the fall seems to bring on momentarily improved fishing. In spring, it slows things up. Snow in late fall will sometimes cause poor fishing for a couple of days.

Chilling of the water below a comfortable level may be the reason. A six-inch snow will cause a sharp drop in stream temperature, and sometimes a rather decided drop. One fall I fished the Madison the day before a snowfall, and the water temperature was 58 degrees. The day after the snowfall, the temperature was 44 degrees. Two days later it was up to 55 degrees. During the period when the stream registered 44 to 52 degrees, I caught not a fish.

Most streams will not show such a quick comeback after chilling. In this instance, the rise in water temperature was due to the input from the Firehole, which poured a considerable volume of 70-degree water into the Madison just above where I was fishing.

I've had some first-class fishing during snowstorms. Oddly enough, some of the time the fish refused the wet fly, but took on the surface with abandon. I remember one case in particular.

It had been a cloudy, still day, somewhat warmer than normal for the time of the year. I got to the stream about 4:00 in the afternoon. About 4:30, a chilling draught moved up the canyon, and it began to snow. In fifteen minutes, it was snowing so hard I couldn't see the opposite bank.

The wet fly wasn't producing, and I could see fish slash-rising, so I put on a big Donnelly Variant, a number 6. By 6:00 it got too dark to see, but in the hour or so that I had been able to see, I took six big fish and was twice broken. At no time was it necessary to cast over 20 feet. If the fly dropped anywhere in the main current, it was taken at once. Top fish for the afternoon, killed and kept, was exactly four pounds, a robust slab-sided rainbow 22 inches long.

At this point, it might be well to mention that the fisherman's attitude toward the weather plays an important part in fishing success. On this particular day, two other anglers were fishing nearby, and their car was parked beside mine on the bluff. As I was removing my waders preparatory to leaving, these two clambered up the bluff and commenced doing the same. I invited them to join me in a warming nip, and we discussed the fishing.

One of the fellows had done very well, the other had not. The words they used to describe the fishing were indicative. One fellow said it was "tremendous," the other said it was "miserable." One had enjoyed the fishing, ignored the cold, the wet snow; the other had been chilled, shivered, and had had a bad time. Guess who caught the fish.

I've seen the above happen so often, I've coined a term for anglers who don't do well during periods of bad weather. I call them "fair weather fishermen." I mean nothing derogatory. It's just a term to describe persons who don't like cold, windy, rainy, or snowy weather. Normally, these fellows don't fish during such weather unless they have a companion who does, and they go along to avoid being called sissies. I can understand their reaction to bad weather, because I, myself, cannot abide hot, humid weather, and usually do poorly if I fish in such weather. Perhaps some would call me a "foul weather fisherman."

It is true that the weather sometimes affects the fisherman more than it does the fish, as the above example shows. One cannot change the weather, the answer is either not to fish in weather one dislikes, try to make the weather work for you, or make the best of the matter.

Making the weather work for you involves such things as "dapping" during periods of high wind. Or, for instance, after a hot spell followed by a rain, you might want to fish a varying-level stream rather than a constant-level. The fish in the constant-level stream probably would have been feeding somewhat during the hot spell, and would not be so much affected by the rain. The fish in the varying-level stream most likely would not have been feeding regularly. The rain, cooling the stream and raising the oxygen level, would revitalize these fish and create an appetite. Thus, they would be apt to feed vigorously.

Conversely, after protracted cool weather, a rain might warm the stream while adding oxygen, and again, the result would be a flurry in fish activity.

The effect of snow is always to chill. The effect is not immediate, and therefore the increase or decrease in fish activity will be spread over a considerable period. The most obvious activity will take place early, before any chilling effect can be noticed. It pays one to fish on or near the surface during the early part of a snowfall. However, if it is a spring snowfall, you might be wise to remain in the cabin, with a hot fire and an Old Fashioned. Fish and fishermen alike are apt to be unenthused by a spring snow.

I have had some good fishing during raging storms—both rainstorms and snowstorms. In general all activity ceases in about an hour after commencement of such a storm, so if you are on the stream when such a storm occurs, you might have good fishing for awhile. On the other hand, you might not, but it will take only a few minutes to tell.

If you are an inveterate fisherman, it pays to have foul weather gear. No matter how enthusiastic one may be, an hour or two in a freezing rain without a rain jacket is apt to blunt the desire to fish.

Some fishermen seem to feel there is something sissy-like about dressing for the elements. Others seem to feel that you're supposed to suffer now and then. This reminds me of a camping trip I took once.

My companion on this trip was a fellow who had more thousands than I had tenspots. He was generous to a fault; therefore, I was surprised to see, at bedtime the first night, that his sleeping gear consisted of one scrawny blanket which he spread on the rocky ground. He snarled and muttered as he wormed around, trying to get comfortable in this rig.

From my downfilled bag atop an air mattress, and ground cloth, I questioned this attitude. His reply was that a man camping was supposed to be uncomfortable; that was why he went.

I hastened to inform this gentleman that it sure wasn't why I went. Nowadays, when I see an angler out in a pouring rain or sleety slush, in a sports shirt or the like, I wonder if he is one of those that think you are supposed to be uncomfortable.

When pondering the possible effect of some weather phase on fish, it is imperative that the "why" be considered. Why does wind or rain or temperature affect fish? If you can't answer the why, or there seems to be no logical reason, it is probable that particular phase of weather affects the fisherman and not the fish.

One must consider several things when deciding what high water does to fishing. One factor is the previous level, before the spate.

If the water is low, but the weather cool, one should expect decreased fish activity. If the water was of normal level, an increase in activity early in the spate might be expected. One must apply the "why" here, because several conditions can exist, and an influx of water would thus have different effects.

If the streams was not deficient in oxygen, then added oxygen coming from higher waters is of no import. If the stream was cool, and the land surface warm, the input of rain would raise the stream temperature. If the stream were warm, the land cold, then the runoff from rain would cool the stream. What effect these changes in stream temperature would have on the fish would depend on what the temperature of the stream had been, and the amount of change.

For instance, if the stream temperature was in the low 50s, a rise of five to ten degrees would induce greater fish activity, all other factors being equal. But if the spate lowered the stream temperature five or ten degrees, to the low- or mid-40s, reduced activity could be expected. Keep in mind the ultimate result of high water.

Under heavy flood conditions, where a stream really roars and pulses, fish usually will not feed, regardless of how favorable any other combination of factors may be. They will be quiet and sheltered until the current has quit battering and shifting the rocks in the stream bed.

The effect of moderate discoloring of water by a spate must be considered only as a side effect. It reduces visibility; if other factors favor increased activity, it will have a beneficial effect. If other factors cause reduced activity, moderate discoloration will be of little consideration. If a stream becomes heavy with mud, the effect is nearly always detrimental.

In moderately discolored water, the angler must consider the decrease in the range of vision of the fish. It may be necessary to choose a fly on the basis of its visibility, and it will be in order to make your drifts closer together. How close together depends on the color of the fly and the amount of discoloration. Only a test can determine this.

Drop your chosen fly into the water, and lower it until it becomes indistinct. If this occurs at a depth of twelve inches, then, in covering a hold, your drifts should not be more than eighteen inches apart. One and a half times the distance at which the fly becomes indistinct is the rule. Remember, no fish will take your fly if he has no opportunity to see it.

If one chooses to fish the fly in heavily mudded water, a fly that will show up well under such conditons must be used. The drifts must not be over a hand span apart, else few fish will see the fly. Black is a good choice of fly color under such conditions, and a large, bulky fly should be used. The Black Marabou streamer is sometimes effective in muddy water. Flies of yellowish, tan, or orange coloration are practically invisible in muddy water. As an example, a size ten Ginger Quill or Light Cahill cannot be seen just under the surface if water is yellow with mud.

Although it isn't common, there have been many cases in which something has upset the balance of a stream, and this has caused a change in the species of aquatic insects inhabiting it. When this happens, fishermen, clinging to their old flies and methods, begin to think the stream is fished out. Actually, a change of fly and tactics was all that was needed.

One case in particular that I know of involved a small creek which, until 1930 or so, had produced spectacular catches of trout.

Then, one fall a disastrous forest fire heavily damaged the watershed. Exceptionally heavy winter and spring rains caused grievous damage to the little stream, silting the riffles, filling the pools, smothering many good insect-breeding areas.

The season following the fire was poor, the next two poorer still. Then the fishing leveled out, but at nothing like its former peak.

In 1941, electric shocking and census reports on the stream indicated the creek probably had more and larger trout than ever before. But the fishermen weren't taking them. Why?

Two big reasons apparently accounted for the poor results. One, the fish were not in their former lies and holds, but were in other areas of the stream which fishermen were passing by. Two, the former dominant gravel-bed dwelling insect species had been replaced by ones that lived in beds of muck and silt.

The result: the fish's food dwelt in a different place and acted in a different manner. The old flies and methods no longer fitted the conditions. The conservation department passed the word around, and today this stream once more has a good reputation.

Most cases will not be so obvious, but all streams undergo gradual change, and the flies and methods that worked on a stream 15 years ago probably will not work now. The fisherman must be alert to these insidious changes, and change his style and methods accordingly.

Changes in the stream bed itself cause a constant migration of fish, because the larger fish constantly seek the better lies. If gravel, silt or other debris fills a good lie, or disturbs the current flow, the fish will probably seek other quarters. These will be the best that his size and aggressiveness can demand. Meanwhile, his former abode will be taken up by a smaller fish, or become barren.

For 15 years, I have watched my favorite stretch of the Madison change. Each fall, on the last day of the season, I leave the stream, confident I know it well. But the following spring I become aware, day by day, that this is not quite the same stream I left in the fall. Small changes have taken place here and there beneath the surface. There has been a shifting of stones and gravel and the lies of some fish have been affected.

One holding area in particular has shifted downstream about 20 to 30 feet in the last ten years. Once, the break in the current that marked the deepening of the bed and the beginning of the hold was just even with the end of a low bluff on the bank. Now, that current break is almost 30 feet downstream of the point of the bluff. The water of the hold is a little shallower than it was. The fish that used to average 1 ¾ pounds now average 1 ¼.

Below this stretch, a once-shallow, unfishworthy riffle has become a medium-deep fast run where I now and then harvest a three-pounder. Just what magic has taken place here, I don't know. I had never bothered to thoroughly explore the place before, once I had determined it to be unfishworthy. Now I am at a loss to explain what caused the change. But, whatever it was, I'm all for it.

Violent floods often rearrange a stream bed to such an extent that in effect a new stream is produced. I've seen this happen on the West Coast, when terrible Pacific rainstorms moved inland while snow was still deep on the upper slopes.

It usually takes several years for a stream to recover from such an event. It also takes about the same length of time for the fisherman to reacquaint himself with the changed stream. Some streams never recover, and some fishermen never do, either, after seeing one of their beloved streams storm-ravaged.

So, a stream cannot be taken for granted. That fishermen will do so is inevitable. They lose touch with their changing stream, fail to change along with it, and one hears the cry "fished out" when, in fact, it's the fisherman rather than the stream who is at fault.

Some fishermen do not feel they can afford the time to constantly reacquaint themselves with a stream. Since the time they can spend on the stream is limited, they feel they must be casting every second. Such men will never become advanced anglers until they learn that study never ceases, and one must constantly be reeducated.

Angling pressure is a factor that cannot be overlooked. It is so bad in some areas that angling cannot conceivably be called "the contemplative man's recreation." What to do in such cases poses a hard question—one that probably will not be answered in our generation.

The thundering herd of anglers, however skillful, will not catch all the fish. The moil of activity will make catching them much harder, and will put them down entirely during the day, if pressure is great enough.

If it is legal, night fishing will partially solve the problem. I, for one, do not care for night fishing, since I enjoy the surroundings almost as much as the fishing. For those who don't mind it, it offers comparatively good fishing.

I prefer, on heavily fished streams, to find spots and areas not fished by the rest of the crowd. Such spots may be rare on some streams, but they are there.

One way to find them is to spend a good bit of time watching other anglers, and fishing the areas they bypass. Examples of such spots are places where brush or trees grow thickly along the bank, and the water is too deep to wade. In general, the more inconvenient a spot is to fish, the more it is apt to go unfished.

Such areas are easily located on many streams merely by noticing where the paths along the bank swing away from the stream. Some of the areas left unmolested may look unfishworthy. Under normal circumstances, they might be. But heavy angling pressure forces both fish and fisherman to seek quieter areas, however unsuitable.

I once took a friend to a stream that hosted a veritable horde of anglers. We spent most of the morning on a low bluff above the stream. Here we could see both banks of the stream up and downstream for half a mile.

Without exception, each of the anglers visiting the stream fished the same spots, and avoided the same spots, as did the others. Few fish were taken.

After lunch, my friend and I went down to the stream and began fishing. We concentrated on the spots the others had avoided. Many of the fish we took were small, but we each took a couple over a pound. Compared to the herd of anglers we had watched that morning, we did great.

I learned about fishing such places when my occupation forced me to live for awhile in Los Angeles. Fishing the leaky-radiator trickles that pass for trout streams in the Southern California mountains was an eye-opening experience. In these streams the fish ran about six to the pound, and the fishermen about a hundred to the mile. Even New York City residents can do better than that.

Some otherwise excellent trout streams are deficient in insect life. These streams get a reputation as being good for the bait or hardware fishermen, but poor for the fly fisherman. I must admit that these particular streams are puzzlers.

They are fairly rare, thank goodness. Neither I, or anyone I know, has ever been able to develop a killing method with the fly on such streams. On some of them, streamers or bucktails do good work, but on others they do not.

The upper reaches of the Yuba River in California are like this. Rarely can one make a decent showing with the fly but the salmon egg and spin fishermen produce decent catches with some regularity.

The only suggestion I have to make about such streams is to experiment. I have occasionally taken fish on the upper Yuba by using flies with an excessive amount of flash or glitter. Also, on occasion, I've taken a trout or two on flies tied to resemble a pair of salmon eggs.

These latter flies are just a little double ball of orange-tangerine chenille on a short-shanked hook. A friend who saw me using this fly once gibed at me.

"Thought you only used flies," he needled, "those things imitate bait."

"All flies imitate bait of one kind or another," I told him.

"I admit this couldn't be properly called a fly, but it is an artificial lure to be used on a fly rod."

"So is a spinner," replied my salmon-egging friend. He had me there.

So, if by some bad luck you find yourself restricted to fishing a stream where insect life is scarce, remember that baits other than flies can be imitated. Remember the fellow with his chamois salamander.

〖16〗

Insects Are The Key

Authorities I have consulted vary considerably in their estimate of what percentage of a trout's diet is composed of insects in the Rocky Mountain West. All agreed, however, that lack of frogs, forage fish, and other meaty items forced trout to rely more heavily on an insect diet than was true in the East.

The above jells with my own findings. I know of few streams in this area that supply minnows, other forage fish, or amphibians in any quantity. I know of many streams that do not contain any of these, and are also somewhat deficient in insect life. These streams, whatever their size, host mostly small trout.

From my own observations, I would guess that the average trout in Western mountain streams dines on insects 90 percent of his feeding time. There will be exceptions to this, of course. However, it is also my experience that western trout feed less on the surface than do their Eastern counterparts. This results in a seeming contradiction. The failure of Western trout to feed often on the surface has led a good many Eastern writers to assume that they feed less on insects. This definitely is in error.

There are several reasons for this apparent paradox. The main reason is a difference in prevalent insect genera. Most Western streams host caddis or stone fly types more than mayfly types. Neither caddis nor stone flies hatch in the manner of mayflies, and this is the biggest reason why Western trout do not feed on the surface to a greater extent.

The above situation also causes many instances of fly hatches that confuse the angler. Just recently I observed such a situation.

An angler from Maryland was fishing along the South Fork. Fish were rising with some regularity; the angler was fishing dry, but with no success.

"The hatching natural is best matched by the Lady Adams, number 10," he told me in an aggrieved tone, "but the trout refuse it. What's wrong with these trout of yours?"

"Try a number 12 Gold Ribbed Hare's Ear," I told him.

I went along, fishing my two-fly cast of blackish green nymph and Hare's Ear dropper. Business was good. When I returned to the car two hours later, the man from Maryland was there, this time wearing a big smile.

"Didn't see those hatching caddis," he told me cheerfully, "until I got to thinking about that Hare's Ear. A fellow can sure get into a rut in this business. I haven't fished a caddis imitation in years because we have mostly mayfly hatches where I fish. Just goes to show." And he went off upstream, whistling merrily.

Sid Gordon surveyed over 350 streams and lakes while doing fishery research and while writing *How To Fish From Top To Bottom*. It was his considered opinion that caddis flies were the predominant insect in more of these waters than were mayflies, regardless of location. Yet most of our writing and instruction is about the mayfly types and how to imitate them.

Partly, this is a hangover from English writers. Partly it is the result of earlier writings by influential Eastern angler-writers who wrote vividly about the delights of dry fly fishing. And partly, it is because the caddis is not as easy to imitate nor as pretty to look at as are artificial mayflies.

Even the experts are not safe from over-emphasizing mayfly tactics. In his excellent book *The American Angler*, Al McClane mentions dry fly fishing a Western lake with the standard dry fly (mayfly) patterns. Fish were rising by the thousands, but he rated not a strike. The next evening the same thing started, and, says McClane—"I tied on Wayne Buzek's big Deschutes Stone Fly and slammed it on the surface. The result was like triggering a shotgun—the water exploded and all my delicate Eastern conceptions came tinkling down in a heap.*

After the rise is over, many a dry-fly man has learned—and this includes yours truly—that he has been fishing the wrong type fly. The same thing happens much more frequently to the wet fly man—again including yours truly. But the wet fly man can seldom

---

* *The American Angler,* New York, Holt, Rinehart and Winston, 1954.

be sure exactly what his problem was because the action takes place unseen. Here is one case where a study of the trout's stomach contents can pay off—providing you catch the trout.

It is almost always better policy to study the insect activity in the stream itself. To be absolutely blunt about it, except when he is spawning, a trout's activities are almost 100 percent dictated by the insects on which he feeds. And it must be remembered, the same environmental conditions affect both the trout and the insects, and in almost precisely the same way.

Here I will digress to speak of something that appears to me to have gone unnoticed by fishermen and biologist's alike. It is this: Poisons which are used to rid a lake or stream of fish also rid the lake or stream of insects. Most of these work by paralyzing the breathing mechanism; the creature, fish or insect, smothers. Fish are restocked, but what about the insects?

I happened to be present one time when a lake was poisoned to remove what was thought to be an overpopulation of chubs. The whole affair was handled badly. There were not nearly enough men or equipment to handle the job. To make matters worse, after the poison had taken effect, very few chubs were found, but hundreds of trout over four pounds came to the surface.

An attempt was made to save as many of these as possible, and anglers were allowed to pick up the dying fish far in excess of their limits.

However, I was more concerned with the insects than the fish. They, too, were dying, literally by the millions.

I approached the biologist in charge. Now, this gentleman had had a bad day. Everything had gone wrong, and when it was discovered the poisoning was in error, a number of anglers had gotten very angry and very verbal about it. Most of their ire had been vented on the man I approached.

When I asked him what would be done to replace the dead insects, he replied shortly that rotenone didn't kill insects. I stepped down to the water's edge, scooped up a double handful of dead nymphs and showed them to him.

He gave me a black look and went storming off, muttering about so-and-so amateurs who thought they knew more than the experts.

This was in 1958. I have kept close tabs on the place since. It took five years for the insects to return, and they have not reached their former abundance yet. The trout, restocked by the thousands, remain small, though plentiful.

I inquire of every fisheries biologist I see about the fact that stream and lake poisoning kills the insects therein. Most have not even given the matter a thought. Some had, but could offer no solution. Two—oddly enough in Louisiana—had, and had practiced restocking insects for several years. They said their records definitely showed that where insects were restocked *prior* to restocking fish, the fish matured earlier and were larger at a given age than where this was not done.

The above, then, points up the fact that insects are the key to fish (trout) growth, and study at the source will prove that they are the key to fish behavior as well.

To return to the theory that fish activity depends on the activity of the insects on which they feed, it is here that water temperature plays its biggest role. I have stated repeatedly that trout are not too affected by temperatures in the high 70s. However, this is not true of insects. Fluctuating temperatures upset a nymph's metabolism, and the reduction of oxygen that often accompanies this phenomenon will, in a great many cases, cause underwater insect life to go into a state of suspended animation. This is very similar to the estivation of certain amphibians and some desert creatures. It is a survival mechanism that takes over to reduce the need for oxygen when there is a lack of it. But the phenomenon occurs only at higher water temperatures.

So, we have a situation where the trout is in a condition of torpor or lassitude, and the insects on which he normally feeds are totally inactive. This results in fishing which is poor, and which is always blamed on water temperatures alone. The culprit is low oxygen content in the water. Agitate the water to get oxygen into it, even without lowering the temperature, and your insects will come alive, and your fish begin to feed.

Naturally, I do not mean to get into the water and thrash it to a froth, although I've often felt like doing just that. Find someplace where the water chutes down rapids, tumbles over falls, beats around rocks, or other obstructions, and fish these areas with the slowest possible movement of your fly. Even in these areas, nymphs will be moving much more slowly than usual, so your fly action should be as slow as you can make it. If you have to add weight to get your flies to drag along slowly, add it. Your trout

Pools, glides, riffles, runs, and cascades. Varied currents, varied bottom structure, very varied insect structure.

may loaf over to pick up an insect but he is not going to dash under these conditions.

No matter what part of the country, or what streams you fish, it pays to imitate and simulate the prevalent nymphs; however, remember, no matter what species you are imitating, under the conditions described, they will be moving very lethargically, if at all.

Speaking of species, just how many species of mayfly, stone fly, caddis fly, etc., do we have in this country? One hundred each seems like a lot; when I started this book I thought there were not nearly so many. I was wrong.

To quote one man who should know, Al McClane, Fishing Editor of *Field and Stream* magazine said in an article not so long ago (July 1966): "there are more than 500 mayflies, 400 stone flies, 400 dragon flies and damselflies, and 800 caddis flies endemic to North America."

Naturally, no one stream holds even a quarter of these. But, and it's a big but, whatever or how many species a stream holds, trout will prefer a certain few over all the rest. It is these few that it will pay to imitate, but it may take considerable study to determine which are the preferred species. Again, here is a case where the study of stomach contents may prove a valuable shortcut.

Once you have identified the preferred species, you still have to know their habits before you can successfully simulate them in the water. Some will be creepers, some scuttlers, very few free swimmers.

Going by books on underwater insects has not helped me much. Most such books are general in nature; what the angler needs are specifics. Some books, even though very good, are confined to one area or even one stream, and thus are not much help, because environment affects insect behavior markedly, and sometimes appearance also.

In a nearby stream, early spring (June in this area) finds two nymphs active before all others. These are mayfly types, alike in structure, size, and actions. They differ markedly only in color.

In the upper reaches of the stream, the nymphs are dark bluish olive in overall color. In the lower stream they are light bronze olive. The hatching duns are exactly alike, however, in all respects.

I believe these two nymphs to be of the same genus and species. I think their color differences are due to environment. The streambed in the upper section is of pebbles and gravel of a general bluish, dark cast. The lower streambed is of large, golden-colored stones, and streaks of greenish volcanic material. I believe the color differences are merely environmental color adaptations of the same species.

However that may be, the important point is that a dark bluish olive nymph imitation works only in the upper section of the mentioned stream, a brownish green pattern identical in size and construction only in the lower. The two are definitely not interchangeable. I have found this true on many streams, and of many wet or nymph patterns.

The duns hatching from the vmphs mentioned earlier, as I said, were identical. They also took lox.ger to hatch than any others I have regularly observed. The fish rose to them very freely while they were hatching but would have no part of any dry imitation I could offer them. This led to the developing of a floating nymph, which I had used for some years in slightly different form.

As originally conceived, this nymph had a translucent body of a small wing quill tip. It was tinted with a thin coat of lacquer, and ribbed with black silk. Another small quill tip similarly tinted was soaked in warm water and bound on by the very tip and then forced upright with tying silk, as a wing. Tail and legs were appropriate barbules of feathers of the proper color.

This took fish, and worked fairly well in the situation under discussion. But the fly was very delicate, not durable in use.

I had some veined wing material of thin plastic, so I used this to make a small pocket or sack to hold the wing quill, which was easily torn off. This improved the wearing qualities of the fly, and the taking quality also. However, the fly still was not very durable, and would usually fall apart after one or two fish.

I finally substituted nylon stocking material for the veined wing material, and started using two small quill tips in the sack, to provide a wing that looked more like that of the hatching fly. This worked fine, and made a better looking imitation also.

I have found that sometimes the fish want this fly more nearly awash in the surface film than at others. To solve this, I sometimes tie the body of regular wool or silk, instead of a hollow quill tip. Sometimes, a hook of heavier wire is used, at other times smaller quill tips in the wing sack are used; but there are limits in this direction.

This fly, which I named the "Natant Nylon Nymph" in 1965, will work when mayflies of almost any type are hatching, as long as it is size-matched. Lacquer of black, blue, green, or yellow is used in tinting, but frankly, the fish seem not to be color selective to this fly when hatching flies are on the water. When it gets a little soggy, a little line grease will fix it up if you don't wish to change to a fresh fly. I recommend it highly as an effective and sporting fly.

For a long time, I studied all the books on aquatic insects that I could find. I learned the scientific names of insects, and then color, appearance, and habits. It did me little good as far as actual fishing success is concerned. I can identify *Isonychia bicolor* readily in the book; in the stream it's a far different story.

This is one reason examination of stomach contents of a feeding trout you have just caught is of little value at the time. If he took the fly you were using, either the pattern or the manner of fishing, or both, is correct. Why change? Also, if you can unscramble a trout's dinner, and say; this is *bicolor,* this is *albomanicata,* that is *dorothea,* you're a better man than I.

You can, however, check color, size, and general appearance of the insects the trout has garnered, for the purpose of comparison, or for making a better pattern.

What you really need to know, however, cannot be found in a fish's stomach. How do these insects act? What were they doing at the time they were taken by the trout?

The only way I know to find out these things is to study the natural insect in action. But, beware. Remember the old story of the drunk who lost his wallet and was diligently searching for it under a street lamp. A policeman came up and assisted him. After a long time with no success, he asked the drunk, "are you sure this is where you lost it?"

"Course I didn't lose it here" snorted the drunk, "I lost it over in that alley."

"Then why were you looking for it here?" demanded the puzzled cop.

"Because the light's better" replied the drunk.

I am reminded of the above story because of an incident I saw last summer. An angler was diligently searching for insects in a quarter-mile-long riffle not over six inches deep. He showed me his find: two small mayfly types, a small black stone fly type, a cased caddis. Then he tied on a small black stone fly nymph and went off downstream to fish a deep pool which had never hosted a stone fly except by accident. He had searched for insects where the looking was easy, not where the fish were. Sometimes it will work. But don't bet on it.

When I first started trout fishing, I thought I had to be casting every second. I had no time, on my precious vacations, to waste studying insects. I studied them in books during the winter. So, I cast and cast, like a man beating rugs, and caught few fish.

I wish I could say the light suddenly dawned on me. It didn't. I started studying stream insect behavior as a result of having more time on the stream. It wasn't until I retired and was able to fish every day that I realized I had learned fishing backwards. If I had started with insect behavior, then learned to cast and fish the fly in imitation of that behavior, I would have been a far better angler far sooner. If there is any shortcut to becoming an advanced angler, this is it.

The state of Pennsylvania, which has done as much trout research as any, or perhaps more, once issued a bulletin wherein it was stated that 10 percent of the fishermen catch 90 percent of the trout. Wisconsin made a similar statement some years later. I believe it to be accurate.

Further, I believe there exist two kinds of experts among these 10 percent who catch 90 percent of the trout. Eight out of these ten I would call empirical fishermen—men who have learned through trial and error, and from others. The other two percent I would call analytical fishermen, who have also learned by trial and error, and from others, but who can and have analyzed the reasons underlying their successes, and are thus the better rounded fishermen.

An empirical fisherman, on his home stream, will consistently catch more fish, and larger fish than the average. But take him to a stream some distance from his pet stamping grounds and he is apt to produce just average results. This is especially true if insects with different behavior patterns are found in the away-from-home streams. On the other hand, the analytical expert will soon commence to make a good showing wherever he may fish. The late Edward Hewitt was of the analytical type of angler.

Here in my area I get to see quite a few of these away-from-home types. The Madison River has been rated by outdoor surveys as the number one trout stream in the nation for several years. Whether it is or not I am unable to say. But this reputation has caused many anglers, expert and otherwise, to visit this area each year, and in the course of the average summer, I see many of them, on the stream and in the tackle shops. Of the expert 10 percent of visitors, about one or two percent catch most of the fish. The others catch fish only when most everyone is doing well. I firmly believe the reason to be that the smaller group takes the time to learn the habits and behavior patterns of the local aquatic insects and to simulate them in their fishing.

I had a long discussion with a visiting fly fisherman on this subject one summer. This elderly gentleman said he was amused to note that other visiting anglers staying at the same resort as he seemed to place all their faith in finding out what local patterns were most used, and employing them without discrimination. Guides, he said, did much to foster this condition, and he complained it was very rare to find a guide who knew anything of insects and insect behavior in the streams on which he guided. One of the leading guides in the area, he snorted, had actually advised him to fish with live bait, sculpins, if he wanted to catch good trout.

He believed that study of insects and their behavior was the best way to insure angling success and he cited two instances among the many he had observed, that caused this belief. Because they involve persons well known and respected in fly fishing circles, I include them here.

Once, many years ago, he had been the guest of a Scottish lord at the same time as Edward Hewitt. They were there to fish, and the laird explained that the streams were becoming overpopulated; therefore each guest was to catch and keep all the trout he was able. There were five other guests, but in three days, Hewitt caught a total number of fish which exceeded that caught by the other five guests. The number was so large, he said, that the laird became concerned, and ended the fishing.

On talking to Hewitt's gillie, he found that Hewitt had spent several hours the first day catching underwater insects and examining them closely. The gillie, a superstitious character, and much impressed with Hewitt's success, had concluded that the insects had told him the secret of catching trout.

The second incident concerned former distance fly casting champion Dick Miller, who, one afternoon, had outfished an entire village of anglers, on a stream which ran through the village. Miller had confided that his success was due to a short but intensive study of the local aquatic insects and their behavior prior to going fishing.

Studying insect behavior is far more difficult than studying fish behavior. I have done some study by going down to the stream bottom in underwater gear and face mask, but most of it has been done indirectly—studying feeding fish, analyzing their behavior and deducing insect behavior therefrom. It is from the latter type study that I have determined that prehatch activity is the thing that excites the fish. The increase in activity, motion, and exposure by insects preparing to hatch acts like a dinner bell on the hungry. I do not mean to imply that this is the only time fish feed, but it is the time that they feed most voraciously, and are least apprehensive, and therefore most easily taken.

Here, also, is a time when study of stomach contents pays off. When you see the just described activity, try to catch one of the feeding fish and open him up. Then you can easily see what type of insect caused the fish's actions, and therefore determine what type of action to give that particular imitation in the future. Also, it should alert you to the type of water in which that insect will usually be found.

In bass fishing with artificial lures, the experts agree the slower the lure is fished, in most cases, the more strikes will be received. This I think is true in fishing the underwater fly. If at all possible, the fly should be moved no faster than the current at the bottom of the area being fished, which will be about one-fifth the speed of the upper current at the same spot.

One of the most consistently successful wet fly fishermen I ever knew actually fished his flies slower than the bottom current. He used as many as six large split shot six inches apart on his leader. He would use enough shot so that the current drag on the line and leader would not move the fly. Then he moved it, usually from a quartering downstream position, retrieving so slowly that the fly crept and crawled across the bottom.

The above method has several drawbacks. Such a rig cannot be cast with a fly rod and line in the usual manner. It must be swung and tossed, with loops of slack feeding through the guides. Distance is limited, the method is tiring, you miss many strikes, you are forever getting hung up. But it will catch trout anytime, any place trout can be caught.

I cannot abide the above method, but have used it at times. On days when I have fished for hours without a strike, I have used this method just to see if fish actually could be caught. It worked.

In an attempt to slow down the passage of his artificial through the hold, another fellow I know fishes directly downstream. He uses shot also, but in lesser amounts, and releases line at the speed he wishes the fly to travel. His method is not as successful, and I believe the reason is that the fly floats up off the bottom. I've had the fly come clear to the top in strong water, with this method, even though weight was used.

I've had best luck using weighted flies, casting almost directly upstream, and keeping as much slack as possible out of, or off, the water. Even so, the drift is too fast for good results in the heavy water I like to fish. Often it is necessary to add fuse wire to the leader to raise the fish I know are there.

In his *Introduction, The Complete Fly Fisherman* John McDonald states there are basically two schools of fly fishermen— imitation and presentation. The imitation school strives for a more natural, realistic-*looking* fly, the presentation school concentrates on *presenting* the fly in a more natural manner.

With due respect to Mr. McDonald, who is, as my father used to say of the late Townsend Whelen, a very sound man, I believe there is a third school, of which I am a member. This third school strives for both a good imitation *and* a natural presentation. However, we of this school are definitely in the minority.

Any manner of presentation no matter how unnatural, and any fly imitation no matter how poor, will take fish some time or other. A feeding fish, where no insect prehatch or hatch activity is present, is rather indiscriminate. He will seize anything that comes along— be it animal, vegetable or mineral. Since a fish has no hands, he must take this material into his mouth to examine it, and thus is sometimes caught on flies that resemble nothing on God's green earth. And since these things resemble no creature, alive or dead, it little matters how they are presented, as long as they come near where the fish is feeding while he is feeding.

In his lifetime, a trout will see scores of different kinds of food items coming down his feeding groove. There will be immature and adult mayflies, dragon flies, stone flies, caddis flies, midges, fish flies, crane flies, horse and deer flies, damsel flies, mosquitoes, houseflies, bees, moths, butterflies, caterpillars, mormon crickets, beetles, grasshoppers, ants, and a host of other landborne insects. In addition, he will see, and probably eat at times, crayfish, frogs, minnows, smaller members of his own kind, mice, perhaps salamanders, even lizards, and of course worms. Some of these he may see only once or twice in his lifetime. Thus he becomes conditioned to grab anything that comes in range on the off chance that it may be edible.

Attempts to explain unnatural or fancy flies have been going on for hundreds of years. I believe the above explanation accounts for their catching fish. Others do not. They insist that their flies imitate minnows, forage fish, etc. The Parmacheene Belle, they say, is taken because it imitates a trout's fin. All I can say here is that I have never seen a trout's fin floating down a stream unattached to a trout, nor have I ever seen a trout nibbling on another's fin. But, I never saw a purple cow, either.

Trout seldom feed for long on one type of insect alone. During prehatch and hatch activity they may, but these conditions occur perhaps 10 percent of the time at most. Nor do trout feed on all the insect types that live in the same stream where they do. Given a choice—the choice which is normally his—I believe the trout will, most of the time, feed on the most prevalent form. Failing that, I believe his next choice would be the larger forms, and thirdly, those most easily captured. On a hard-fished stream, the latter may become his first choice, simply because it requires less exposure to the thundering herd of fishermen.

McClane has said our mayfly species number 500, the stone fly, dragon fly, caddis together number 1600. Therefore, these outnumber the mayfly three to one. Yet, in the East, I agree with the angling writers that the mayfly type is the one most taken by trout. Angling pressure, the very numbers of fishermen on the streams, is the major reason, I believe, although I think the ratio is a little more like two to one in the East. The mayfly's prehatch and hatching activity make him the most easily captured of all underwater insects at this time. Further, he is present in more types of water, especially in those places where the fish may hide from the angling horde. Angling pressure, then, has conditioned the trout to take the mayfly as the staple of his diet.

So far, in this chapter, I have concerned myself solely with aquatic insects, and underwater activity. However, land-born insects form a fair portion of a trout's diet, and we must consider them apart from the usual dry fly patterns and methods.

Firstly, as Ed Zern says about folding a road map or a moose, let us consider the grasshopper as opposed to the mayfly. A live mayfly arrives on the water as lightly as a thought, and so should the imitation. On the other hand, the grasshopper arrives with great abandon and a juicy splash, and so should his imitation. Further, the mayfly rides without drag, but the grasshopper kicks and struggles across current, and it is not a mistake to so handle his imitation. Make sure, however, that the leader does not interfere or add to the fuss.

I have often had trout refuse a cricket, grasshopper, beetle, or even crane fly imitation floating without drag, only to smash lustily when the fly was given some semblance of struggling. I have many times seen trout slash the water to a froth in pursuit of large moth types skidding dizzily along the surface. So, when we present a terrestrial insect imitation, let us do so with thought and style and not in the manner of a mutant mayfly.

In finishing, I am aware I've left much unsaid, but I do not believe that it all can ever be said, nor do I believe theory and instruction can ever completely replace practice. I only hope to have stimulated thought somewhat, and perhaps provided enough information to cause someone to want to learn more, and to tell us about it. I hope to be around to hear about it.

Index